WILLAMETTE RIVER GREENWAYS

Willamette River Greenways

NAVIGATING THE CURRENTS OF
CONSERVATION POLICY AND PRACTICE

Travis Williams

Oregon State University Press   Corvallis

Cataloging-in-publication data is available from the Library of Congress.

ISBN 978-0-87071-144-2 (paperback)
ISBN 978-0-87071-145-9 (ebook)

∞This paper meets the requirements of ANSI/NISO Z39.48-1992
(Permanence of Paper).

Oregon State University Press
121 The Valley Library
Corvallis OR 97331-4501
541-737-3166 • fax 541-737-3170
www.osupress.oregonstate.edu

Contents

For my wife Erica; my daughters Eleanor, Frances, and Portland; and my many friends and family. For my always supportive parents as well, who have been steadfast even when my navigation was a bit off the mark.

I also thank the many people in my profession I've had the honor to work with and learn from over the past twenty-one years in the same job. It has been fantastic, and today many of them are not only colleagues, but friends as well. Here is to the continuing journey.

Preface

Over the past twenty-one years I've had the privilege of working to protect and restore the Willamette River as riverkeeper and executive director of Willamette Riverkeeper, a twenty-five-year-old nonprofit organization that works to protect and restore the Willamette River's water quality and habitat. The organization takes a watchdog approach at times, but also has a wide array of programs, from habitat restoration and land acquisition to toxics reduction and river education. From my experience as a professional advocate and environmentalist over those years, I've gained a particular perspective related to policy, politics, science, and verifiable facts. Over time, as with anything, grappling with issues and situations that are often not black or white, but instead gray, has been a reality as well. This book is not about a particular job or background, but some of the experiences, and the lens through which I view them, are shaped by my chosen profession.

Regarding the inadequacy of particular people and agencies and their inability to better protect water quality and habitat, I identify some but leave the identity of others open to interpretation; I do not feel that I need to name names. Hopefully you, reader, will trust my experience and perception of what is right. At times the failings of those in positions of power to protect a river like the Willamette are entangled with the inadequacy at the heart of the institutions in which they serve, whether city, county, state, or federal. The same strengths and limitations hold true of private businesses.

Over my riverkeeping years, I've seen very excellent people make tough decisions to help the Willamette and other natural wonders, and I've witnessed abject disinterest by a range of people who should have known better, a sprinkling of managers, agency directors, county commissioners, legislators, and others who in one way or another chose inaction, or chose to look the other way when a problem was at hand.

I've also seen this disfunction in a few other organizations, working on matters of habitat restoration, fish passage, water quality, and other issues. At times the pettiness and small-time politics have been astonishing; thankfully, those instances are generally few and far between.

All in all, my time working for the Willamette has been a valuable opportunity that has leaked far into my personal life; at times it can be hard to separate the two. Frankly, my world is permeated with the Willamette, but that is something I embrace. Clearly these chapters emerge from my work/life perspective, which should surprise no one: that perspective is shaped by years of experience, research, investigation, ongoing learning, and a great many days exploring the whole river system.

In my time working on the river, I've met many amazing people — and to all of you, I appreciate your interest, generosity, and mostly good humor. Here is to making progress for the natural world over the next few decades. We surely need it. See you out there!

Introduction

Imagine a large river, winding its way north through a verdant valley. The view is full of lush floodplain forests, interspersed with backwaters and meandering channels everywhere. The trees are mostly deciduous, with black cottonwoods, Oregon ash, a mix of willow species and other native trees and shrubs swirled together in a dense and beautiful assemblage. Large, and fairly shallow, the river winds among these forested lands and past the massive gravel bars moved and shaped by the river in seasonal bursts. Here and there people make their way: a drift boat, then a canoe, and an occasional person trying their luck fishing along a gravel bar. Further on, a hiker makes way along a riverside trail, enjoying the quiet of the river and seeking out the birdlife. In this place, a feeling of peace is interwoven and supported by the sound of the rippling current.

Looking at this river from above, we see the forest extends for at least a mile on both sides of the river outside of the valley towns and cities, and in a few locations the natural floodplain reaches out into thousands of acres. Once in a while a road provides a viewpoint of the river, allowing those traveling by pavement to get close. Most often though, roads and highways are miles away.

Here and there, small groups of people can be seen camping along the river, empty canoes and kayaks marking their places, along with small brightly colored tents perched along the gravel bars. Campfires alight at dusk as the stars make their way against the descending sunlight. Soon laughter and conversation drift through the twilight. Traveling northward, you could see a similar reality along the river for more than 150 miles. Although this vision is not yet the reality, it is not such a difficult reality to imagine; in fact, a similar vision was brought forward more than fifty years ago for the Willamette River.

In the summer of 1966, then state treasurer Bob Straub made a monumental proposal to establish the Willamette River Greenway—a concept centered on the protection of the river and its floodplain lands, and on providing recreational opportunities. The concept was firmly planted on the idea of increasing public lands for recreation, all along the river. Back then the proposal was big—a grand gesture that would provide multiple benefits for people and for the health of the river.

Bob Straub's proposal, in its truest form, was very straightforward—to create a long strip of public lands along the Willamette River, starting south of Eugene and stretching north to the Portland metro area. The Greenway would span more than 180 miles and would be filled with large developed parks and scenic viewpoints, replete with natural areas centered on the needs of fish, mammals, and birds. The plan would also be based on the purchase of land from willing sellers.

This proposal from Bob Straub came during his campaign for governor in July of 1966, against a very worthy opponent, Tom McCall. The 1960s had seen a surge of public interest in the Willamette River's health, mostly centered on water cleanliness. Similar attention had been applied to rivers across the United States in those days, usually those experiencing well-documented impacts from urban areas full of industrial pollution and, later, those affected by agricultural inputs en masse, such as fertilizers, herbicides, and animal waste.

The growing awareness was due in part to Tom McCall's time as a reporter in the 1960s. In 1962, McCall's documentary for KGW in Portland, *Pollution in Paradise*, provided a clear reality check for what was ailing the river. The documentary was filled with images of the river's dirty water, its surface fouled with oily sheens. Fish kills were also in evidence, along with the conversion of habitat along the river. The picture was heinous, representing the worst of how people had tarnished the natural world of their home river. Images of huge industrial pipes spewing dirty water into the river rounded out the reality check provided by the documentary, capped off by images of farm machinery dispersing chemicals to orchards and other crops, demonstrating the magnitude of pollution in the world of the early 1960s. *Pollution in Paradise* raised awareness of the ills affecting the Willamette River and helped spur further action to decrease pollution.

McCall's advancing of awareness of the river's ills rested on decades of effort by other people who had advocated for a cleaner river, admonished industry and municipalities for their tepid efforts to improve conditions, and carefully documented water quality and degraded habitat. For many years, people had witnessed the Willamette being polluted or modified by projects like the Willamette dams, which changed the very nature of the river and the species supported by it. Their collective efforts had had an effect, helping bring critical attention to the river's plight; *Pollution in Paradise* was founded on this long-standing work.

McCall's work as a journalist helped propel him into politics, leading him to run for governor a few years later. The public pushed, and those in power took action to require better treatment of industrial wastes; municipal treatment of sewage was greatly improved as well, in part as a result of *Pollution in Paradise*.

Straub was also taking an active role in thinking about the Willamette River's health and had supported river cleanup efforts as state treasurer. Prior to his campaign for governor, he had been lobbied by Karl Onthank, a professor at the University of Oregon who had a deep history with environmental issues in Oregon. It has been said that Onthank provided both Straub and McCall an abundance of information about the concept of a "greenway" along the Willamette River during the early days of their campaigns for governor. Whether Straub learned of the concept from Onthank or from another source, he would be the first to submit a Willamette Greenway proposal to the public.

In what seems a refreshing notion today, Tom McCall—from a different political party—immediately endorsed the idea of the Willamette Greenway. This gesture is pretty amazing by today's standards, in stark contrast to our age, in which political campaigns and politics generally have become so venal and, in some cases, replete with deception and lies. At that time, two people of different political parties could agree on something, and move forward in support of it, without their actions being overly evaluated as a political ploy or a clever, overly vetted campaign device—not subject to a range of focus groups, or deemed by pundits on one side or the other as a smart tactic, but simply a reflection of the time.

From what we can see from the historical record, the Willamette River Greenway was a good idea that a lot of people supported, and Bob Straub and others injected it into the world of public discourse, knowing that people loved the idea of a healthy Willamette River. We should also remember that this proposal came during a time when thinking big translated to action in Oregon. One need only consider the bottle bill passed in 1971, and the Oregon Beach Bill passed in 1967. These were big ideas;

they represented the best of forward-leaning pieces of legislation that set new standards for environmental health and public access.

In recent years in Oregon, I'd argue that such efforts have been lacking. These days, it seems, any bold idea thrown into the world in support of the environment soon becomes carefully stripped of all meat and meaningful sinew, its flavor drained away, and the original structure of the idea, concept, or grand plan demoted to an unrecognizable blob. If you'd prefer the vegan or vegetarian version, the tofu is thrown in the pan with the cabbage, but there is little heat, and most certainly the sauce has no flavor. Forgive this metaphor gone awry but, having worked in the environmental realm for the past twenty years in this state, I've gotten a pretty good taste for all the ways things are done—and undone.

Too little effort has been made in holding the line against pollution and forwarding healthy habitat. One might even argue that basic, smart, and meaningful proposals are quickly knocked back by money, ideology, and myriad political trade-offs. The wider needs of human health, clean water, clean air, and healthy lands are set aside for the short-term political posturing of the day, of which both parties are guilty.

Looking around the whole state, in regard to clean water, healthy air, and healthy lands, many would agree that we've lost something even from just a handful of decades ago. It might also be said that some of the "green" accomplishments have obscured long-standing ills that remain to this day. Today, state agencies that protect wildlife and people have smaller and smaller budgets, in a time of major population increases throughout much of Oregon. The department in charge of enforcing rules for how agriculture is conducted is, at the same time, the industry's major promoter. Frankly, that setup makes little sense—it is a framework not designed for good results for the environment as a whole. The Oregon Department of Environmental Quality (Oregon DEQ) has scant resources, with budgets that have been slashed repeatedly over the last two decades; too few of the good people who work in these agencies are able to do their jobs as they should be done. The same holds true for the Oregon Department of Fish and Wildlife. In most cases, people are seemingly afraid to make basic decisions for fear of blowback.

For some, the idea of enforcement—taking action when rules and standards are violated—is for some reason a tough concept to openly approve. The same can be said even for merely meeting a specific standard. A popular trend has been encouraging voluntary efforts to make improvements to the environment, rather than implementing firm requirements that set meaningful, measurable standards that must be met. In some cases, the infrastructure to effectively implement such laws at the state level is broken, or has been warped by time. I'm thinking of the Clean Water Act, especially, along with other good examples.

Witness the long list of expired permits in the last twenty years that regulate wastewater discharged into public waters each and every day. Since the state has lacked the capacity to renew these permits, they just continued to operate under the existing, old requirements—hindering the ability to apply new technology, new consideration, or new approaches to old problems. As in many cases with the Oregon Department of Environmental Quality, a lawsuit was needed to make it take action, in this case renewing the expired permits. At times the agency won't enforce standards, so entities must threaten to sue, or actually sue, the violating polluter or entity to protect the natural world.

As for the Willamette River, the big river surrounded by the majority of Oregon's population, it continues to be plagued by many of the same issues that have affected it for decades. Over time, new issues have arisen as well, lessening the import of the strides taken in the late 1960s and 1970s. In a great many ways, we've taken far more from this river than we've ever given back. The river has been the receiving water of vast amounts of treated effluent and untreated waste over the decades, and up to today. Vast floodplains along the river have been converted into cities and agricultural fields.

Lowlands along the river are known generally as floodplains; it is intuitive, really. You need not be a long-standing scientist to quickly understand that water rises, and when it spills across a low spot, it flows outward across the adjacent lowlands. In most cases these lowlands have received such a regular pulse of water over time that small channels appear, and backwaters fill up. Sometimes seasonal channels emerge, only to disappear or greatly reduce in size in the spring or early summer.

Seldom do natural seasonal floodwaters spread out across the floodplain—and when they do, the water now spreads onto mostly agricultural fields. Sinuous depressions near the river, the old channels that still exist here and there, are in many cases resting just out of view from the main channel and lack the water that once inundated them for many more days a year.

Long ago, many of these lost channels were cut off from the main river, to keep the river at bay and allow people to do business in both urban and rural areas. Back in the day, it was all about keeping the river in a tight channel, spurred by the not-infrequent reality of floods that affected anything built or grown adjacent to the river. Keep it dredged for navigation, relegate it to one main path as much as possible, and build the riverside up to withstand floods—that was the approach. For some, that remains the approach.

Today's river scarcely resembles the river that once flowed large and regularly across the floodplain, sustaining myriad native species. Today, thirteen major US Army Corps of Engineers dams restrict the river's flow from the main tributaries, though on occasion these dams can't keep the water back, and we are all reminded of the river's true nature of seasonal flooding. The Corps' dams have produced major negative results for fish and wildlife, resulting in listings under the federal Endangered Species Act. These dams block passage for native salmon seeking return to their spawning grounds, and likewise for juvenile salmon working their way downriver. On most days the amount of flow "given" to the river is altered, sometimes daily, by the Corps dams. In addition to these

A gorgeous beaver dam backs up the slight current of the back channel.

Corps dams, other private dams exist as well on the river's tributaries large and small.

Over the years, the number of people living near the Willamette has only increased, and the impact from people has increased as a consequence. These changes have occurred in the face of earnest efforts to improve the types and amounts of waste allowed into the river system. Now, I know, some out there will say, "The river is in much better shape than it was back in the 1960s." A case for that argument can be made in relation to measuring dissolved oxygen and bacteria levels because, by those measurements, conditions are generally better than they were decades ago. If that is our measure, then things are likely typically better from south to north. Much of the progress that occurred after the 1960s was related to traditional water quality measurements.

As time has gone on, we have learned a lot about what healthy rivers need. We have also learned a lot about the need for quality habitat and healthy floodplain lands. We've also learned about the impact of pesticides and a host of other chemical inputs to the river. We simply know more today than we knew definitively in the 1960s on those issues.

A good analogy might be comparing our understanding of the science of river health to our understanding of the science of human health. Although some of the approaches and assumptions made in the medical field fifty years ago are the same employed today, an entire world of understanding has opened up in the last few decades in most every field of medical science and treatment. We have a much more vast and detailed comprehension of neuroscience; we have a better understanding of how to treat cancers of many types, and major advancements have been made in treating type 1 diabetes. We know more about gut microbiota and, frankly, most any disease or ailment one can think of. New knowledge and approaches have been applied to how medical conditions are treated, from the hardware used to the medicine prescribed. It is just a vastly different world in many respects.

The same can be said for our understanding of river health. Ironically, even though we know more today than decades back, our rate of change has been all too slow. The lack of response to new knowledge reminds me to some degree of people who continue to smoke cigarettes even though we now know that such careless action adds monumentally to cancer risk. The approach of our government agencies, as well as the private sector, has too often been to look the other way when it comes to implementing new environmental science—instead, they just keep smoking their policy-and-enforcement cigarettes.

One need only look at our expanding understanding of the effects of toxic pollution, which affect the health of wildlife and people, or to our understanding that a healthy river needs to be connected to its floodplains—that natural conditions must be in place for any expectation of relative health. As should be expected, our knowledge of these things has expanded over the last fifty years. Unfortunately, change has not always resulted from that knowledge.

Decades ago, the impacts of dams on the Willamette were not fully recognized—from blocking native fish runs to altering the temperature of the river—and these effects have been too little addressed, even though we now know their negative consequences. Likewise, the effects of the loss and modification of the Willamette River floodplain habitat was too little understood; pollution from runoff was overlooked, from the industrial yard next to the river to the endless gallons of herbicide spread across tens of thousands of acres of riverside lands. Everything that runs across the thousands of square miles of adjacent agricultural and urban land can run into the Willamette or one of the tributaries. Strides were made and momentum was created, but over the decades, loopholes were created and exploited, and the backbones of those who might have done more were too soft. Now, decades later, many people and organizations are trying to deal with these issues, but judged against the job at hand, it is not too far a leap to say that progress is *still too slow*.

These things that affect the health of the river ecosystem matter—a lot. Fish, birds, and mammals that have lived along and in this river for thousands of years are having a hard go—*due to us*. Flushing our chemicals and wastes, whether through pipes or across fields, does little good for clean water and healthy habitat. Imagine for a moment being a fish, swimming in the Willamette and breathing in the toxic waste of our economy, swirling about in nanograms per liter of everything from bifenthrin and atrazine to diuron and DDT. Some of these are legacy chemicals and some are new with ongoing use. Taken together, these myriad artificial substances may well have long-term consequences on the natural world that are presently too little understood. It is not a significant jump to wonder at the potential health implications for a fish, breathing in water polluted with these substances.

Today the Oregon DEQ has far too little capacity to test and screen for pollutants in our waterways, a fact proven over and over in the past twenty years. The agency that promotes agriculture does far too little to curb agricultural impact on water quality and habitat. Even under a settlement to improve fish passage at the major dams on the Willamette's tributaries, the US Army Corps of Engineers moves at what seems like a snail's pace, yet lacking the persistence of a common snail, to make improvements. The sense of urgency that might normally be present in such cases seems decidedly absent.

At the macro level, we are indeed "Slobivious americanus," as Ed Abbey put it well, and this designation certainly applies to what we've all done to the river. What I reflect on is the idea of the Greenway program as something conceptually much more than a linear strip of public lands along the Willamette. Don't get me wrong—having that kind of natural riverscape originally proposed by Straub along the Willamette would be amazing, and a huge improvement over what exists today. Frankly, it is a proposal that needs to be reinvigorated for the future health of the river (more on that later). In a sense, the word "greenway" is also a powerful concept through which to evaluate and understand the many historical and current aspects of environmental health in Oregon.

We plug the river's tributaries, we pour poison into the soil that eventually flows to the main river. We release our tens of millions of gallons of industrial waste to the river and we do the same with municipal wastes. We spray chemicals from the air onto agricultural lands, onto forests—and we spray them into the water too. We now have myriad invasive species to contend with as well. So, what "green ways" do we have left?

Although there have been, and are, major issues facing the Willamette River, there have also been some bright spots for river health in the last twenty years. We can look at increased restoration of habitat here and there as a gain. Even so, much of this restoration has occurred on lands already owned by the public, rather than on lands that have been recently acquired for the public. We have also made improvements to polluted sites, such as the cleanup plan for the Portland Harbor Superfund site. In time, the work to remove toxic sediment will begin, and other areas will be covered with clean soil. We can also look at the increase in low-impact recreation facilitated by the Willamette River Water Trail as a gain, with thousands of people over the years spending time traveling the river in paddle craft and visiting public sites along the river. To be optimistic, maybe the cup is 20 percent full of clean water—yet at the same time, we are collectively trying to limit that bit of clean water from spilling out as we run the equivalent of a major rapid in a canoe!

If we reflect back to the 1960s, how does the vision for the Greenway stand in light of today's Willamette River reality? What do the "green ways" of Oregon have to do with the river's health, and that of the rest of the state? How does climate change interact with historic and newer approaches to natural resource management?

It would seem that Oregon in many ways has not kept up with some of the other states around our nation in our "green ways," and it may be that we have fallen behind in multiple areas. Apologists for how Oregon has related to natural resources have been many over the past few years. Over time, the excuses have become commonplace: "Yes, I know we've slipped, but given where we are, this is the best we can do." Such a statement might have been generated by most any state agency, or by a host of politicians, typically relating to the funding situation in the state and federal governments. Yet there are those who make it their jobs to enable the status quo. Some state senators and House members can care less about clean water and healthy habitat, especially if dollars are in the conversation; I recall these representatives more than once not even pretending to listen to testimony from experts in some subject areas. Their minds were already made up. Similarly, related agency heads and policy directors are frequently pushed by lobbying professionals who make their living seeking to erode efforts to protect water quality, restore habitat, and clean up polluted sites. Often these promoters of their particular company or sector work to do the least that is legally required. I've seen manipulators of a variety of sorts working for industry to maintain the status quo, or to degrade it—if for just one more legislative session. One can also call into question the many appointments to boards and commissions that oversee agencies, from forestry to agriculture, which, in most cases, have helped maintain the status quo. Business as usual is business as usual, and we have been in that mode for far too long in Oregon. The grand ideas of a former day have long since faded.

This sweet little island is really a few islands, with the river pushing its way through here and there.

   In terms of clean water, clean air, functioning rivers, and healthy forests and their related watersheds, too often these days Oregon leans on its past accomplishments: the Bottle Bill, the Beach Bill, the effort to clean up the Willamette River in the 1960s and 1970s—all meaningful efforts that occurred multiple decades ago. Those monumental efforts made a difference for Oregon, but trotting them out as ready icons of Oregon's green ways in the present is nonsensical. Since then, new rules to protect watersheds have been few and far between. We've seen legislative efforts to better understand which pesticides are being sprayed onto the landscape, and at what volume, be undermined and underfunded. We've seen the Oregon DEQ so depleted that to have an onsite inspector look at a wastewater discharge that is violating its standards has become a hard-to-staff project. We've also seen a lack of additions to the Willamette Greenway's natural areas—with no plans to work to add more land. The list could go on.
   Not lost in any of this is the reality that the Willamette River Greenway came into being, and—for all its liabilities and challenges, many of which are discussed in this book—it offers much to explore. Along this

river are a tangled collection of lands, a ragtag fugitive fleet of floodplain assemblages, a mishmash of watery forest properties that have somehow been allowed to exist in a natural or somewhat natural state. Many of these properties are central to the Willamette River Water Trail, a project that helps educate people about how to access the river, and how to travel it for a day, a week, or more via paddle craft (learn more about the Willamette River Water Trail at willamettewatertrail.org).

These properties are worth exploration, and can be revealed to some degree to you, the reader of this book. Perhaps more importantly, exploring these properties provides a good feel for how the Willamette River is today, how we have not always done well by it, and how, in many ways, we continue to neglect the river, and many other natural attributes in this state. I chose to write about this river system because I know it better than any other part of Oregon, and also because it is subject to so many environmental impacts. Whether riverside development in our cities, altered flows from large dams, repurposed riverside lands that no longer provide healthy floodplain function, or the array of chemicals found in the water—the impacts are widely seen, and felt. So, how do our greenways stack up?

My intention is to provide a picture of some of these places and issues, shedding light on them from my experiences of these riverside lands and my two decades being immersed in the policy and political realities that relate to the Willamette, and Oregon generally. You will also read of a few of the people I've encountered over the years along the river. This narrative does not aim to tell you about every one of them—or every experience, place, or person of note. I also do not explore every action that negatively affects the river's health, so forgive me for that in advance.

In the same vein, this book will most thoughtfully *not* highlight every Greenway property along the river. Frankly, some places should remain unspoken of. If you want to explore them, maps and descriptions are easy to obtain, and you can do that on your own. What I hope you will realize is that these properties need friends, and they need new contemporaries. They are also a very useful lens through which to understand other greenways that greatly influence the health of this river, and of this state.

A hopeful notion is that some of what readers will discover in this book will be new information. Over the years it has become clear that the Willamette River is not a central focus for a lot of people in the Willamette

Valley, or for the State of Oregon. If anything, thoughts of the river are generally negative, based on bits and pieces of the river's common narrative of historic pollution and ongoing issues. At the same time, I think, once you gain a bit of additional perspective about this place, many of you may become Willamette lifers.

I've been fortunate to be able to work on the Willamette, doing the same job, for a couple of decades now. A lot has changed in the world in that time, yet the needs of the river are much the same. This work has been accompanied by the usual stress of running a small nonprofit, with all the glamour such work entails (you small nonprofit folks know what I mean). At the same time, I've been lucky to be working for the good of the river all that time, in the same organization and in the same job. I have met some truly awesome, dedicated, smart, fun, and creative people each and every year in this river work. Many have become good friends, and that is a blessing (you all know who you are). The luck of that is never lost on me.

Luck has certainly played its role in my life, and every day I'm able to spend on the river I grew up on—whether doing hands-on work or recreating here on my own time—I feel exceedingly fortunate, and grateful. As I put the finishing touches on this manuscript in 2020, it is also not lost on me that white privilege has played a role in my career, and that of many others, and I'm cognizant of that. Working to get more people from myriad backgrounds into the environmental, conservation, and recreation fields is critically important.

It is also essential to acknowledge the first peoples who called the river home for thousands of years, in places that people now "own." The notion of ownership of these riverlands, and those beyond, is ironic to say the least. It has been gratifying to make good friends among the members of the Confederated Tribes of the Grand Ronde and other first peoples, who have helped advance critical work, and to have great working relationships with them.

Over the years I've developed a perspective on the river that may not be shared by all. I'm happy to mark progress where it is real, but I have a strong feeling of discontent about this river's health—and about the status quo. An evolutionary leap is needed. To borrow part of a lyric I've always loved from Neil Peart and Pye Dubois, perhaps I'm "always hopeful, yet discontent" about this river and other related things in the natural world. That seems to strike the right note for me.

I am writing the final words of this introduction in early September 2020. We've seen a year like no other in my lifetime. From much-needed efforts to address racism after the death of George Floyd and many others to the global pandemic, the year was marked with stress, anger, and anxiety for many. It was also marked by some of the worst national leadership in history on a number of levels. As for many in September 2020, my neighborhood was covered with the yellow-brown smear of smoke from nearby forest fires that have thrown an entire region into turmoil. People have fled their homes, others have provided shelter for friends, family, and strangers. Tens of thousands of others sheltered indoors against the worst air quality conditions ever seen in the Willamette Valley and other parts of the state. Homes, businesses, and entire towns have been wiped out.

Clearly, the months and years ahead will see thousands of people working to rebuild and start over. Others will leave the region entirely, acknowledging the altered environmental conditions caused by climate change. On the heels of all this, perhaps the perspective of this book—the observations of one person over a period of years—will seem like one lone person yelling in a storm. Or perhaps this collection of experiences and thoughts can open a new door, or at least a view, to a part of our world that still retains a lot of beauty and promise—one that is worth our thoughtful care and attention.

All I hope is that you will come away from reading this collection of thoughts and experiences understanding a bit more about the reality of this river, Oregon's rivers in general, the broader environmental reality in Oregon, and across the country and in the world. I also hope you come away wanting to do more for Oregon's natural areas and environmental health—and wanting to improve our green ways at all levels. I hope too that, like me, you will bite into the Willamette Greenway concept and help grow it further—on the Willamette River, along some other waterway, or in some other green fashion. At the end of the day, protecting and expanding our greenways will help protect the natural world—and therefore, in fact, the human world—for the long haul.

Somewhere near Norwood, Oregon, late fall 2020

1
The River's Gift

I had been my whole life a bell, and never knew it until at that
moment I was lifted and struck.

—Annie Dillard, *Pilgrim at Tinker Creek*

Just beyond the sound of urban traffic, down a short lane to a primitive
parking area, another world is revealed. Trading the whirr and rush of
automobile traffic for the sound of water and the rustle of old cottonwoods in the evening breeze, you can see the lively current pushing itself
northward on the big river. The flow moves on, under the watchful eyes
of osprey, cedar waxwing, great horned owl, coyote, and deer. On this
June evening, the light is bright, illuminating the leaves on the tall cottonwoods, Oregon ash, and the expanse of willows at the river's edge.

Combined, the light wind and chattering of leaves mesh with the
flowing river current, a natural murmur that insulates against the intru-
sion of outside noise. Cars, sirens, and the dull thrum of persistent traffic
in the distance seldom penetrate the boundary of the sound generated by
the river and the creatures that live along it. On my first few visits to the
Willamette River Greenway, the sense of being *elsewhere* was paramount.

Indeed, there are moments in one's history when it does seem a kind
of bell is struck for the first time, perhaps when a window opens into a
world. A new place, a new idea, or a new approach—these instances and
more can be signaled by that bell, marking a moment when something
critical has been understood or experienced. A feeling, a sight, a real-
ization, and one can finally see what has surrounded them all along, or
become immersed in something entirely new.

For some, a first walk in a floodplain forest adjacent to a sweet river
running high from mountain snowmelt might trigger that feeling. The
view of the shimmering trees descending to the river's edge, bordering
the moving water. For others it might be that first effort to capture a trout

in the shallow current, waiting patiently among the bright splendor of the water on a late summer evening as line and rod work their magic. In a moment of fun and relaxation, it could be the first swim in a cool river pool on a hot day, soaking up the refuge from the heat. For others, that sense can arrive from the first foray down a river, paddling a canoe, moving through and with the current, placing the sleek hull of the craft on the fast flow and feeling the current carry it along. For still others it may crystalize in a momentary glance across the wide rippling river, spotting an eagle pair perched high in a cottonwood tree. For those acquainted with the dealings of rivers, connections like this abound—each one ringing that bell anew.

Forests along the river's edge can provide buffering from other things. A trail among the trees creates growing insulation as you walk, a break from noise, a blanketing and beautiful assemblage of forest growth and blue-green water. Here and there the two reach into each other in what appears at times to be nature's perfect artistry.

A trail, recently dampened by spring rain, weaves soil and root through the forest. The primitive course edges around fallen trees and ever closer to the river. It may leave you at the top of a gravel bar, where the enclosed woods give way to the open and lowest part of the river's floodplain. Here the view is broad and outward, where willows dot the gravel bar for hundreds of meters, swaying in the wind.

Current swirls and ripples, moving quickly downstream. Somewhere out of sight, the distinctive call of Canada geese can be heard. Across the wide channel, a tall stand of old cottonwoods push upward, their formidable line extending far downriver. Upon first sight, they seem a towering wall of newly leafed green—their vibrant leaves having just emerged into the spring light after a long, rain-sodden winter. These trees have seen storm after storm pushing over the coast range and into the wide valley, unleashing immense downpours. In some months these downpours brought the river many feet higher, sending pulses of flood flows deep into the riverside forests.

A few minutes lingering on the gravel bar shoreline can bring you completely in. Ageless and ancient, the river world quickly appears. The human grind of the everyday is weakened, diluted, and, thankfully, can even seem eliminated at times. While this blanket of riverine protection is thin, and does not provide full coverage in every situation, more often than not the stir of the water, the flex of the big trees in the wind, and the sound of a kingfisher moving along the shoreline can provide temporary refuge.

Years ago, a spring canoe trip along the Willamette made that first riverine bell ring for me. With my tent situated along a gentle backwater on a Greenway property, I had found a perfect spot for a bit of quiet on a near-moonless night. The lake-like water was still, and the skies clear. Bright blue and twinkling, vibrant starlight from the far stretches of the universe could be seen reflecting in the pool. Light from thousands of years ago glancing off millions of water molecules. Diamond-bright and shimmering, the sky and river's surface were ablaze. Starlight was cast with a sprinkling of blue, maybe even a deep old blue, where the difference between the colors was undefinable—some morphing waves of energy that my human eyes could barely discern spread overhead. Just above the water's surface, the dark silhouette of the cottonwoods rose across the channel, tall and textured, meeting the vast expanse of cold air, and finally emerging into the star-washed sky. Just then, a great horned owl burst from the canopy.

I leaned forward, my skin tingling in seeing the silhouette, the moving outline of this great bird. Sure, they can be heard with some regularity all along the river, but to see it burst forth under the starlight meshed with a sliver of moonlight was something else. With its visibly large head and determined flight path, the great bird headed across the river to the west, toward another collection of cottonwoods.

Reassuring, and even soothing, a feeling that was old and basic gripped me. This was the river, and the land that it had morphed over time—pushed and pulled repeatedly over the years by the power of water. On this night I was lucky to be there to witness that owl, to rest against the river rock island shaped by the seasons, and to consider what was, and what might be. I sat there on the river rock beach, my spine tingling. In the moment, my senses seemed to gather the movement of the fish in the pool in front of me, looking upward as they sensed the radiance of the stars. In the moment, I felt the gathered movement of the moths, spiders, and aquatic insects moving about, newly awakened by warmer days. I couldn't care less if they were crawling over my legs—only glad that they were there, and alive. It seemed that I could sense the beaver swimming just downriver in its nightly routine, leaving myriad sticks removed of bark—evidence of a solid dinner. All of this rang true in what might have been ten minutes, or an hour, as the coolness of the night settled in. I was on a river that was always the same, but always becoming, different—each and every moment, and each and every day. The sound of the bell was very clear.

A nice example of Greenway lands includes the Oregon Parks Greenway property I was camping on. The property had been there for quite a while, perhaps many decades or even longer. According to the available maps, this spit of river rock, silt, and sand had changed shape from decade to decade, had been trimmed and slivered from year to year and, more recently, turned into an island from high flows pushing through a neck of land. Even so, it was still in roughly the same place. Somewhere along the way, willow had taken hold, along with the mid-sized Oregon ash tree, and then the larger black cottonwoods. Over time, the beautiful small rounded rock had been ground and pushed by the river into longer slivers of gravel bar, holding the mass of root wads and trees, ever shaped by the rise of winter and spring flows, then receding to show the geomorphological work of the seasons.

Back in early 2001 on a cold winter day I paddled the Willamette River from Whitely Landing to Marshall Island, a stretch of about eight miles just downstream of the cities of Eugene and Springfield. Whitely is a small park in the Willamalane Park and Recreation District, accustomed to a wide range of uses by a wide range of local residents, situated on a small back channel of the Willamette River. The side channel creates an island, creatively named Confluence Island, sitting as it does generally at the confluence of the McKenzie and Willamette Rivers.

Whitely Landing, visited by a slim and continuous stream of people, is in essence a bit of forest with a small parking lot and crude boat ramp. It seems home to the midday restless and those seeking just a bit of quiet and beauty from a small side-channel park. It is also a sweet place to get on the water. In summer the shallow channel ripples with currents, all colored by the swath of willows on either bank. You can dip your canoe paddle into the water and hit gravel just a few inches down. Even so, the impact is immediate: it feels lively and full of life as soon as you get on the water and begin to move away from the old ramp, the sound of an approaching car replaced with the gurgling of current and the calls of birds. This summer scene is far different from my first approach here.

In 2001, when I got on the water here for the first time, the back channel was deep and fast, but not to a dangerous degree. I had brought a colleague, and we met a new volunteer in my organization's work, Barbara May. She had said her many years of river travel and many trips on this stretch would guide us down the modest eight miles to the takeout at Marshall Island. Needless to say, the swirling brown water was invigorating, especially in our canoe. As ever, Barb was attentive to the needs of the paddlers new to this stretch, yet at the same time the river was near the height of its seasonal power.

The mid-January day was an interesting choice. I'd paddled a few times here and there over the years on the Willamette and other rivers, but had started in earnest as a canoeist only a few months before this trip with Barbara. On this day the current was thick with oatmeal-colored silt, and the river was high below the McKenzie River confluence—meaning it had a lot of water. I can recall having an immediate respect for the power of this thing, though I had a kernel of optimism that a person could canoe down it safely.

We were dressed mostly appropriately for the adventure, with warm boots, dry tops, pants, and lots of layers. In hindsight, I likely should have had a drysuit—or at least a wetsuit. Of course we also had throw ropes and the requisite personal flotation devices (PFDs), more widely known as life jackets. We also had backup gear in dry bags, just in case of an unplanned swim. These are the basics of river travel, key equipment that must always be present in order to have the best chance at a safe trip.

When we poured out of the side channel after just a few minutes on the fast flow, Barbara May guided us as we zipped down the undulating, swirling mass of brown water of the Willamette's main channel. Our canoes—Barbara in her whitewater solo canoe, we in our long tandem—glided past massive cottonwood logs blocking most of the channel around an island and past portions of the river that boiled with energy, where the water seemed to erupt from the river bottom and gurgle upward into a blurry mass.

We skirted strong eddy lines just inches from the hulls of the canoes, avoiding those portions of the current that contrasted drastically with the main direction of flow. Typically, these areas of the river flowed upstream along one side or another, to some point where the water was diverted back to the main current. If we had hit these strong reverse currents, they might have sent the canoe sideways or, worst case, sent us for a very cold swim. We sought to keep our pace slow and thoughtful, and took great care to stop and look ahead at anything that might prove to be problematic.

You may not know, but "swirlies" are quickly appearing small whirl-pools that generate a bit of force, depending on their size. They can have the same dramatic effect on the hull of a long canoe as the more typical eddy lines. With high water on a big river, you can see swirling masses of water on the left and right, sometimes allowing you a small passage of current in between. Arising from significant river flow, the shape of the channel bottom, and other variables, swirlies can nudge your craft from side to side with varying degrees of force. Here and there the swirl-ing currents move across the river channel, providing little notice for the oncoming paddler.

To the newer paddler, swirlies can be pretty disquieting. Realistically, they are a complete and nearly perfect example of the power and unpre-dictable essence of the river. Here and there these swirlies, seemingly independent creatures, move from side to side across the river's surface, making a game of sorts of predicting where they will appear, or even of simply spotting the nascent eruption in time to maneuver the canoe. When I first started paddling, years back, these feral, unpredictable forces of the river gave me pause—and they still do at times. I soon learned they were an interesting part of the mix—as long as I kept my paddle in the water, pulled on it, and kept my hips loose, the canoe would proceed just fine. Left, then right, the bow of your canoe or kayak might budge a bit, but as long as one is calm and keeps paddling, the course will keep true. The sheer physics of this process still amazes me.

The upwellings have a similar vibe, yet give more pause to the paddler. Out of the blue, the volume of flowing water, combined with the shape of the river channel and more, suddenly cause a flow of water to spout directly to the surface—at times this boiling uprising is many feet wide.

The source of the flow—from snowfields to the east and rain-drenched coastal mountains to the west, with nascent flows joining into creeks, then to small rivers swelling with winter rain—is wide and charged with energy. Untold billions of molecules flowing all around, guided one way and then the other and directed and bounded by a particular type of substrate, or knocked sideways by large rocks. At times it may be one converging cur-rent against the main flow as the water rises, then giving life to slowly spinning whirlpools and upwellings on a cold winter afternoon.

River traits like these can play with your imagination, which can be very healthy. What if one of these sent me and my paddling partner into

The fog lifts slowly from the river at Harkens Lake.

the drink, into the swirl of fast-moving high water? It isn't that hard to imagine swimming along looking for any opportunity to get to the riverside without getting caught on a large log or root wad extending out of the water—which could spell a bit more than just a bad day. Of course, another very real possibility for a person in such a situation is becoming hypothermic. Needless to say, that swim, if successful, could take a very long time when the water is rushing at high flow. If you reached the riverside, would you be able to find your gear? Would you be hypothermic and lose judgment and overall function? Would you find help in time to stave off the cold if you weren't wearing proper high-water gear, such as a drysuit? At any rate, a very healthy respect for the power of the moving water is a smart thing to cultivate as a river traveler. It is especially important to always hold on to that respect for the river.

In all, the reality of traveling a river acquaints one with the sheer power of the natural world. It seems that most people have some instinct that kicks in, telling them that a moving river is a place to both appreciate and to be very wary of. Any flow of water, high or low, should provoke those sentiments, yet when the river is high and the energy is above the norm, it may trigger an additional sense of a human's place in the wider world.

That day, in the misty gray of the early year in northwestern Oregon, our crimson-colored canoe wove downriver, riding the current and dodging the swirlies. At one point we pulled the canoe along the rounded rock of the riverside, jumping out to move past a log that had come to rest across a good portion of the river's current, steadily pulling the line from the front thwart of the sleek craft. We had chosen the smaller of two channels, the one to the east, because the main western channel was clogged with root wads, full trees, and pieces and bits of a conglomerate forest that had found its way to the river via the tangle of tree roots. Within these cottonwood root masses we could see soil and rock held tight by the roots.

Here and there full trees could be seen with their root wads extending above the water's surface—tree roots as intermingled masses of flexible fiber fingers still cradling a concentration of rounded river rock and mud. Sometimes the roots seemed part of a massive forested hand that had dug down into the riverside earth to reveal what was below. Now the hands were reaching upward, so close to, but so far from, the riverside soil from which they had come.

As we paddled onward, we surveyed the river lands around us, always looking downstream to be sure we avoided any obstacles. Here and there water rushed into small openings along the gravel bars, pulsing water through the willow, recharging small backwaters that had not seen much flowing water in months. Historically such rise and fall was simply natural, and it occurred with regularity before the dams were constructed and greatly changed the nature of the river.

After a while, we reached a broad and slower stretch, where all around us a discernible sizzling sound could be heard. The vibrating noise seemed to push through the hull of the canoe as we paddled. It didn't take long for us to realize that we were hearing the noise of millions of bits of sand and pebbles being whisked along the river bottom.

Like food in a hot olive-oil-coated skillet, the sizzle went on, rising up through the brown roiling water and into the hulls of our canoes. We bent our heads toward the water outside the boat and listened—we could hear it sizzling all around. I could only imagine the millions of particles moving along the river bottom, pried from the riverbed somewhere miles upstream, then swirling downriver and, miles later, interacting with a hundred million other particles, reach after reach.

With the ripple of the current, the swirl of the energy of the dark water on that day, the rise of the mist across the dark water—we were hooked on canoeing that river, and that is all there was to it. So, blame Barbara May, and her guidance, consideration, advice, and river knowledge—on that day and after.

With nearly every river trip I've done in the last twenty-one years, that riverine bell continues to ring. Even in the COVID-19 time we've all endured, I was able to elope with my family and one friend to get married on the upper Willamette. With that, the river has clearly kept on with providing its enduring gifts.

2
The Willamette Greenway Program

[The renewal of the Willamette River Greenway program will] bring
us back to the original intent of the program: to preserve this magnificent resource now and in the future.
> —Bob Straub at the Oregon Capitol, January 13, 1975, quoted
> in *Standing at the Water's Edge* by Charles Johnson

Go back more than fifty years, to July 1966, when then state treasurer Bob
Straub, running in a tight gubernatorial election against Tom McCall,
made the first formal proposal for the Willamette River Greenway. The
proposal reflected growing interest and discussions going on around the
United States about the need to protect rivers, to provide public land
where people could recreate, and to provide habitat for wildlife. This
was an important moment for this river—but the history of this river runs
even deeper.

For thousands of years, the people of today's Willamette Valley were
the Kalapuyans; it was their land. Other groups of native peoples also
came across the mountains from the east side, and over the Coast Range
as well. The people practiced seasonal patterns of gathering food in established places, trading with other groups and making a living. Descendants of these people are still here today, represented in the Confederated
Tribes of Grand Ronde and other confederations. Of course, over time
the lands were wrested away, taken piece by piece in treaties that were too
often not adhered to. Generally speaking, the Indigenous peoples had a
far different relationship with the land and rivers than those who ended
up taking them—including a sense of stewardship and a deep knowledge
of seasonal patterns, inherent abundance, and ecological balance.

Looking at the Willamette and its tributaries, these rivers and the
creeks above them provided salmon, trout, water, lamprey, and myriad
resources for food, travel, and shelter. At one time of year huckleberries,

as we call them now, were sought high up in the mountains, and the endless acres of these delicious berries beckoned people from afar. At other times fish were running upriver in abundance, and people knew to be there to collect their share of the harvest. All the timing, the places, and the patterns of these yearly activities were well known and passed down from generation to generation. From time to time, fields were burned to assist with hunting, or to better enable certain plants to be harvested.

In the early 1800s, the first white visitors made their way to Oregon from overland, some of them to the Willamette Valley, and they gained some of that knowledge. Over time many of them sought to cultivate the lands, and they worked to keep things at bay that may have threatened their effort to grow crops. That basic drive, not singular to one place or another, pervades a lot of settled places and many cultures. If something appears threatening, whether a scary potentially predatory animal or a river at flood, people tend to want to protect themselves and the things they value.

Imagine the wolves that once lived in Oregon, in the Willamette Valley itself. They were widespread before being extirpated by the newly arrived white visitors from the East. Unfortunately, the fate of the wolves was tied to the practicalities of livestock predation but also, perhaps more so, to a wider fear. As we've seen in recent times, fear and misinformation tends to do strange things to people.

What I've gathered about the river over the years is that enough people saw the Willamette as an unruly feature that it had to be dealt with, it needed some degree of taming—or perhaps even the eradication of its natural, wild ways. Others may have simply found the river dangerous, and sought to trap it in their own way, to reduce its potential to impede a particular way of life along its floodplain.

I am reminded of Roderick Nash's book, *Wilderness and the American Mind*, which provides a detailed analysis of how the natural world was viewed for centuries by European settlers and how much of that perspective was based on fear: fear of wildlife, fear of weather, fear of raging floods, fear of the dark, and fear of the unknown. It seems that, in some ways, such thinking has stuck with us. For most who travel the natural world today, healthy respect is on order, whether scaling a mountainside or paddling a fast current. Respect and due consideration are essential and perhaps, in the right conditions, even a bit of fear. But at times a line can be crossed, and fear can fuel actions and practices across a wide spectrum.

Intertwined into any discussion of how we think about the natural world is the notion of control. In an effort to exert control, some would like to curb the wild, to lessen the simple unpredictability of what comes at us. Most definitely, it seems to me, a great measure of control is exerted by people in regard to the Willamette: the many examples, approaches, and instances of efforts to control the river can be documented going back 150 years or more.

Mile after mile in places along the river you can see riprap, the somewhat orderly artificial collections of large rock stacked or piled along the riverbank. Sometimes these layers of rock go on for hundreds of meters, then appear again around the next bend where the river, as it is wont to do, presses against the outside bend. Any river naturally erodes in these places, or spreads outward—making them prime targets for landowners trying to stave off loss of riverside soils by riprapping. Usually a combination of public and private funds have paid for these projects over the years.

Riprap is used to keep the riverbank from eroding, and to keep that wild river off the adjacent land, whether farm, city, or industrial site. Combine these rocks with pilings and related wood structures at the top of the riverbank, and you might be able to keep that river at bay, at least for a while. Of course, in urban areas, much larger and more engineered approaches can be found; over time though, even such fortifications have been no good against flooding. Heck, the river has flooded since time immemorial. For most of history, the river used to spread out across its floodplain, that expanse of low-elevation riverside lands, for many miles. Filling vast sloughs and backwaters with the pulse of winter and spring flows was the norm. Year in and year out, the river took its natural course.

People settled along the river. Sometimes they settled just high enough to not be subject to the annual flood of the river, with perhaps only part of their property under water for a time every year. Perhaps land was cleared that was inundated with the river's flow once every four or five years. That kind of inundation would potentially create problems for agricultural fields if the water stayed for a while, and for homes and other buildings. As a consequence, the logical sequence would be to push back against that flow, push back against that thing that caused you, your family, and your livelihood some kind of harm.

If you look at an aerial photograph of the Willamette River in 2020, or pretty much any time in the last seventy years, it is easy to see the lay of the land and water. The vast array of floodplain lands that once connected with the Willamette have been largely separated from the river. Riverbanks have been armored by stone, some dumped and some carefully placed along the river's edge. Instead of hosting a verdant mix of willows, red osier dogwood, and other species, these denuded expanses of riverbank become a lifeless reach of gray rock. Whether on the big Willamette, or a tributary like the Long Tom that flows slowly from the southwest, the lack of vegetation offers little for wildlife and provides no shade to cool the river. These long-held practices can be difficult to let go of—becoming a habitual embrace of engineering against natural river function.

At the same time, the natural essence of the river, those wide floodplain forests, backwaters, and channels, has been greatly altered by development of large agricultural enterprises, and the ability of these lands to absorb portions of high-water events has been greatly diminished. Instead of protecting these water-absorbing areas near the river, people replaced them with hardened structures that in many cases do little to protect against flooding.

Agricultural families, cities, and others worked to protect their property against threats from the river, real or perceived. Even today, this river-versus-the-people perspective persists with some people who live along the Willamette. When the suggestion of a network of public lands along the Willamette was made, some saw this new threat from the river as not about floodwaters, but instead about the flood of people who might spread out across riverside lands.

A greenway is commonly known as an assemblage of natural riverside lands of various sizes, clothed in "green" vegetation and providing some measurable habitat for birds and mammals. It might be a thin strip of trees or something more substantial that is clearly established habitat for fish and wildlife. *Merriam-Webster* defines a greenway as "a corridor of undeveloped land preserved for recreational use or environmental protection." Such a definition seems universal and easy to comprehend, with scale as the main variable differentiating one greenway from another. A healthy greenway might include trees, shrubs, and wildflowers, an abundance and range of native plants that provide a place to live for a variety of species. The definition rests with our idea of the composition of "green."

An eagle's view of the Harkens Lake area.

Public ownership of such lands is usually a given fact, almost implied in the overall idea; or at least public use of most riverside lands would be a given. These outcomes speak to how a community approaches the larger philosophy of the public trust, and the related doctrine that finds its way into environmental law, and is also expressed in how organizations establish and maintain public lands.

The origin story of the Willamette Greenway can be told in a variety of ways. The basic idea—to protect and secure land along the Willamette River from just south of Eugene all the way up to the Columbia River confluence—was hatched in the 1960s. Today the program exists through both the Oregon Parks and Recreation Department's holding of riverside properties and local governments administering rules regarding development along the river. Although the combination can be a little confusing, each of these aspects of the Greenway has its roots in Goal 15, one Oregon's nineteen land use goals. In 1973, Senate Bill 100 was passed, creating Oregon's land use planning system, and the Land Conservation and Development Commission (LCDC) and its related department. In 1974 the state's land use planning goals were created by the LCDC. Not long after, in the summer of 1976, Goal 15 was created to deal with protecting the Willamette, which permanently established the Willamette Greenway. Thankfully, even this watered-down version of the original Willamette Greenway vision has been valuable for the general public and for river health.

Webb Bauer's doctoral thesis, published in 1980, chronicled the history and intricacies of the Willamette Greenway program. In Bauer's time, the Greenway was a fairly recent policy conundrum. His work was detailed, engaging, and reveals a lot about the program's inception, early missteps, and internal issues. Bauer had worked for Oregon Parks, including during some of the early work to establish the Greenway.

According to Bauer's thesis—and documented as well in the wonderful book *Standing at the Water's Edge*, a biography of Governor Bob Straub by Charles Johnson—Governor Straub made the first formal Willamette Greenway proposal in 1966. Some also maintain the Greenway was Straub's idea. At the very least, Governor Straub is credited with putting forward the first defined proposal for the Willamette Greenway, with emphasis on recreation and conservation, while he was still state treasurer during his gubernatorial campaign against McCall.

Professor Carl Onthank of the University of Oregon has also been credited with the original Willamette Greenway idea. Some say Onthank put the idea forward in the mid-1960s and forwarded information about the Greenway concept to both the Straub and McCall gubernatorial campaigns. Whether Straub or Onthank originated the idea, both put a lot of energy into the concept.

Senator Maurine Neuberger introduced a proposal to Congress, published in August 1966, to draft a plan to create public lands along the Willamette. The plan proposed that funding be allocated from a federal open spaces program toward the purchase of private land to create natural areas and public trails. In 1967, *Northwest Magazine Sunday*, an insert of the *Oregonian*, published an article titled "River Rediscovered," describing the Willamette Greenway concept. When McCall heard of Straub's proposal, he wholeheartedly agreed with it and supported it.

When McCall won office in 1967, he sought to put the Greenway concept into action. Few people understood the complexity of the task at hand. In a 2014 phone conversation with me, former state parks director Dave Talbot described being in a 1967 meeting with Governor McCall and Glenn Jackson, the powerful chairperson of the Oregon State

Transportation Commission. Talbot recounted, "Governor McCall came in, and said to Jackson, 'Okay, how do we get this Greenway program going?'" Talbot continued, "Jackson looked at me, and looked at McCall. Then Jackson pointed to me and said, 'Have him do it.'" In this way, Dave Talbot, director of Oregon Parks, was tasked as the point person and agency to move things forward for the Greenway.

Soon it became clear that the idea of the Willamette Greenway would be hindered by misunderstanding and disagreement with local landowners along the river; fear had a role to play as well.

As Webb Bauer establishes so thoughtfully, clearly the values of the urban people who embraced the idea of the Greenway created fear among the rural landowners along the river. The idea of having people from the city floating down the Willamette and potentially trespassing on their lands created a lot of angst among a group of people who were used to doing things the way they had "always" been done along the river—at least in their recollection. Of course, both rural and urban people had been using the river for recreation for decades already.

The varied stories and perspectives of the Willamette Greenway, how it came to be, and how people sought to implement it is multilayered and spans several years (it may be argued that the effort has taken decades). One strong narrative pitted the local landowner against a hungry government that would stop at nothing until all the land along the Willamette River was turned from private to public. Of course, the reality is far more nuanced. Straub's proposal called for a long series of public lands along the Willamette, with the State of Oregon acquiring private land from willing sellers. Some agricultural interests did not like that idea at all.

The proud history of public lands in the United States ranges from wonderful state parks to federal lands that allow for a vast amount of recreation. Public use of the natural landscapes across the United States for recreation is well documented and much admired by many. Examples include our National Park System, our great rivers, and even unprotected public lands that allow backpacking, hiking, birding, fishing, hunting, and more. The level of support and engagement was clear: the US government and state governments had a legitimate role in creating natural areas and parks and protecting these lands for the long term. The difference with Straub's proposal was that most of the riverside land in question was at the time private—not all of it farmed, but private all the same.

The vision Straub introduced comprised a long stretch of land on both sides of the river that would be in the public domain. Some areas would have scenic overlooks open to car traffic, while others would be signature parks with a range of uses. Other parcels would be accessible only from the river, serving chiefly as natural habitat or primitive camp-sites. Purchasing lands from willing sellers was seen as the main avenue to securing private lands for the public. The notion that private landowners would go along with the program and recognize its value to the river and to the public may have also been in play.

In the early days of the program, under Governor McCall, the State of Oregon created a grant program to help cities and counties purchase lands along the river, utilizing federal funding. The greatest success was seen in Lane County, where a Friends of the Greenway organization had been formed and a good amount of energy had been generated as a result. Soon, multiple properties were in, or moving toward, public ownership. Natural areas such as Camas Swale, Mount Pisgah, and Elijah Bristow State Park were acquired. What seems pretty clear, though, is that less support for this program was found among local riverside landowners in the rural stretches of the mainstem Willamette.

According to some agricultural landowners, at some point in the process of meeting with landowners, state agents from the Department of Transportation (which oversaw Oregon Parks at the time), mentioned that the state could also purchase the land from unwilling sellers, utilizing the right of eminent domain. Indeed, this was an option for the state, as for many states and the federal government. Unfortunately, this notion stalled the accelerating Greenway canoe, pushing it immediately up onto a gravel bar and leaving only a small current to support the original Greenway vision. As a result of the suggestion of imminent domain, some agricultural landowners organized and worked to put a stop to the program.

In cities, progress had been made in applying the state grants program to help acquire parks, but no large parks had been created by most counties along the river. As a result, according to Bauer, the state prioritized establishing five focal parks as large visible symbols of the Willamette River Greenway park system. Ultimately, four of the five were created, and today these parks provide many benefits to the river, and to people.

By the time Bob Straub became governor in 1974, the original vision of the Greenway that he had put forward had been drastically reduced.

The Oregon land use planning system had just come into being in 1973, and the Greenway was shifted to that process for its formal establishment and assumed continuation. The same state legislation that had created the land use planning system, SB100, prevented the use of eminent domain on agricultural lands along the Willamette. Representative Norma Paulus, who later became state treasurer, is credited in part with making this aspect of the legislation happen. Ironically, after her death in 2018, a Greenway island upstream of Salem was named after her.

Land Use Planning Goal 15, which today we call the Willamette River Greenway program, was a fantastic development on a number of levels, but definitely did not capture the original vision of creating significant public lands. Today, Goal 15 is providing rules for riverside development in every county along the river, and related but separate rules in the cities. The Oregon Parks and Recreation Department (OPRD) holds the legal authority to purchase lands along the Willamette from willing sellers, and the ability to receive donated lands.

Much of this story is well told by Bauer, and in Johnson's *Standing at the Water's Edge*—both are must-reads for Willamette River "lifers," providing detailed accounts of the Willamette River Greenway's history and the various versions of the story. Bauer completed his very interesting work in 1980. I looked him up, hoping to talk to him after I found the thesis. Tragically, he died of cancer not long after he completed it, still in his early forties. When I spoke with his wife Chesta in 2015, she was happy to know that anyone would be interested in the Willamette Greenway program—and his thesis. She told me how hard Webb had worked on the project. She also indicated that he was not all that happy about how the state sought to implement the program, with many missteps, in his view.

Webb Bauer deserves a lot of thanks for the time and energy he put into his work; it is a pretty amazing accomplishment. His contribution to understanding the Willamette's public lands is fantastic and will continue to be a lasting work. Charles Johnson's account is also great, providing a much broader view of Bob Straub than just the Greenway. It is worth a read of multiple levels, especially as an account of a politician too often overlooked in Oregon history for his environmental accomplishments.

Goal 15 continues to shape policy today. In recent years, things have moved in a positive direction for the Greenway. Not too long ago, in the

Beautiful Pacific willows emerge from the gravel bar.

early 2000s, Oregon Parks and others almost wanted to stop using the name Greenway. Apparently the influence of a few agricultural landowners along the river had made the agency a bit timid about using the name, and like-minded people in other areas picked up on that. Some folks also appeared cowed by a few landowners who still have issues with the aspirational program and its launch, and who feel that using the name is problematic—even into the 2000s. In my time working along the river,

I've met many people who have made statements like, "We need to stop using the name Greenway. It gets too many people riled up." That sentiment pervaded parts of OPRD for years. Thankfully, the name Willamette Greenway is again enjoying fairly wide use.

Oregon Parks and Recreation Department had been conditioned to hearing from local landowners that the department doesn't take care of

The author happened on this Greenway sign that had floated downriver more than sixty miles to downtown Portland. Perhaps it was a sign of the Greenway's renewal and persistence.

their land and does too little for their Greenway properties. Years back, even a few who worked in conservation and restoration made similar statements. A landowner I spoke with in 2014 was worried about a new property where dispersed, leave-no-trace camping was allowed on the Willamette River, on an island accessed only from the river. He said his sister lived in a house on the upper end of the island's back channel. Having just read of some of the history of the Willamette Greenway program, I was honestly shocked when this landowner used language that might have been more appropriate in 1968 than in 2014—though frankly it was never really appropriate.

The landowner said his sister was worried about "river people" who trespassed, and that they sometimes carried guns. The word "undesirables" was used more than once. "We just want to know what is planned there, so that we know there isn't a threat." It felt like a flashback to decades past, with these folks still parroting the sentiment from more than fifty years before. It brought back to me the old quote, "The more things change, the more they stay the same."

The funny thing is, since that time I've heard that sentiment again from another private landowner. Part of me can understand the well-cultivated effort to keep the river at bay and, in essence, to control some aspect of it. That desire has deep roots (puns intended). At the same time, a lot has changed in this world over the past few decades, so part of me is mystified at the inability of some people to let go of such overused notions that have little to do with reality.

Unclean, unscrupulous, possession-seeking, law-breaking, ill-intentioned river travelers—now that is an interesting image! Ah, here's to the river pirates, gathered in the back eddies of fevered imaginations. Strange images circulate in that pool of thought: of canoes, kayaks, and driftboats flowing along the river's surface, all planning their takeover of a piece of Eden, each sporting a Union Jack, displayed proudly, moving with the current, upriver to down on a regular basis. Picture these pirate craft, floating barely above the water line, packed so deep and heavy are they with the loot captured along the river from private landowners!

Evidence is scant that river users of any type create any kind of havoc on the Willamette Greenway. More often, problems arise when people enter properties from the landward side, not from the river. The only loot these river pirates are after is peace and quiet, the call of great blue

herons, the dive of osprey, and the gentle sound of cottonwood trees
rustling in the wind.

After my initial shock, I was able to talk to the man about the hundreds
and hundreds of paddlers I've known who travel the river, the same kinds
of folks who spend time on a lot of rivers and lakes in the United States
and Canada. To a person, they just want to chill out and enjoy the peace
of the experience. Whether conservative, liberal, socialist, or independent,
the many people I have led down the Willamette over the years are by
and large an excellent lot. Heck, some even worship the flying spaghetti
monster, but at the end of the day, it is almost universal that the people
who regularly canoe, kayak, or driftboat simply love the river and have zero
interest in bothering anyone. On the other hand, all too often, river travelers encounter the sounds of farm equipment droning all night, gunshots
from private properties, loud music, incursions into rustic public property
by four-wheel-drive vehicles from the land, and more.

Protecting these beautiful places, and the water and the lands around
them, is usually front and center in the thinking of river travelers. Further,
cleaning up the messes of other people is the usual mode of operation for
those who use human-powered craft—such as removing the plastic bottles
and other debris that get flushed downriver from the cities during high
flows, or cleaning up after thoughtless people who visit sites by land.

Those who spend their getaway time in canoe, kayak, driftboat, or other
craft, seeking out the peace of the rippling current and slow-moving pools,
have little interest in disturbing anyone else, and that respect certainly
extends to private landowners. Of course, issues can occur at certain sites
or stretches of water: I'm thinking of some of the Willamette River tributaries, such as a stretch of the Clackamas that is very popular for certain kinds
of water travel on the hottest summer days. In those cases, people who
reflect the lowest common denominator can make ill-conceived decisions
that result in trash and debris left along the shore. This was vividly demonstrated during the summer of 2020 along the Willamette, as new groups of
people found riverside areas—with a percentage of these folks leaving all
manner of waste during their thoughtless outdoor delirium.

Nearly universally, people who travel the river also love the river. I told
the rural landowner that they sure as heck don't carry guns (if anything,
only duck and deer hunters do that), and such hunters are a relatively
small group along Willamette floodplain.

The sentiment that private landowners do a better job managing their lands than their public counterparts has been repeatedly expressed over the years. This falsehood is put forward largely to advance the political agenda of restricting public lands along the river to a minimum. In fact, a survey just a few years back on the mid-Willamette for invasive weeds found that the lands owned by OPRD, Oregon Department of State Lands, and other public entities were in better condition than nearby floodplain lands that were privately owned. Along these lines, over the years an almost comical notion has been put forward by some: that there is a dearth of agricultural land along the river. Again, this notion is advanced by a few vocal people concerned about having any more agricultural land adjacent to our rivers being "taken out of production."

Most people can recognize the value of farms, and the hard work invested by people who own them, manage them, and provide physical labor. In addition, many of these farms are growing valuable food crops, with some transitioning from growing grass seed to more interesting and sustainable food crops. Among these are even some organic growers! Realistically, there is no lack of agricultural land in the Willamette Valley, and most certainly no lack along the river.

In fact, if you fly from south to north, just a few hundred feet above the Willamette, most of what you see, to the west and to the east, is a vast expanse of agricultural land, interspersed here and there with pockets of forest green and the occasional Greenway property of a handful of acres. More often you see a thin line of trees along the river, with vast fields on the other side. In some cases, the fields go on, literally, for miles. So, let's once and for all dispel the notion of a lack of agricultural land; transitioning some of these lands from agriculture back to natural floodplain habitat does not represent a threat to agriculture in the Willamette Valley. Instead, it represents another kind of production, a type that is essential to healthy river systems and overall ecological health.

In the last few years, the OPRD has begun to recognize the Greenway program in a bolder fashion and has lost most of its trepidation about using the name Willamette Greenway. The agency, as poorly resourced as many others, has sought ways to better manage their lands, from large parks such as Champoeg park to vast natural areas such as Luckiamute Landing State Natural Area. The department has also done long-term planning for some sites and has invested time and resources in a way that the program has seldom seen previously. Some have even talked openly about Bob Straub's proposal, and the value of these public lands for wildlife, and for people. It seems the effort to separate all of us from this important environmental accomplishment from the early 1970s has failed—and the use of the name Willamette River Greenway is regaining new momentum.

What seems pretty clear is that, over the years, some riverside private landowners have gained a sense that their use and vision for the river is more important than that of others, and that "public" use of the river and public lands along the river is a threat. Although not all agricultural landowners reflected this view, when the original Willamette Greenway idea was hatched, some landowners had visions of "hippies from Eugene" floating down the river, causing havoc on public lands and trespassing onto private lands, doing all manner of hippie things. In reality this didn't happen, of course. The idea, though, persists to this day along certain parts of the Willamette.

The Oregon Parks and Recreation Department is devoting increased resources to the Greenway program, which has been gaining strength over the last few years. Arguably, the agency is not devoting *enough*, but there has been a positive uptick. In 2015 a property just a few miles upstream of Salem was purchased to honor former transportation commission chair Gail Achterman. A group of friends and the Trust for Public Land sought to give the land to OPRD but, in a telling moment, OPRD refused to take the property, thanks to the local Farm Bureau disliking the idea of public access.

The handful of public lands on the Willamette, compared with the tens of thousands of acres of agricultural land, demonstrates a pretty rich irony. I understand OPRD's need to obtain funding from the Oregon legislature, but the deference paid to long-held powerful interests in Oregon, however contrary their interests are to a mission or a need, continues to be a problematic aspect of the Greenway program that needs to be addressed and fortified moving forward.

What is striking is that, over the past few years, outside interests have been exerting more power than ever before. Now we have relatively large corporate interests buying up land in the name of "safe, green investments," even with agricultural operations that are not all that green. Others are hell-bent on transitioning acreage to hazelnuts, while others are looking toward viticulture. Change is clearly afoot.

3
Blue Ruin

> In our contemporary world, an ethic of concern for the nonhuman
> arrives not a moment too soon.
>
> —Gary Snyder, *A Place in Space*,
> "A Village Council of All Beings"

Greenway properties offer a lot, and there are some fine examples that
show us why they are important both for the ecological stability of the
Willamette River system and for recreation. Blue Ruin is a Greenway
property on the upper river, about nine miles south of Eugene. One
can really take off with pondering the origin of the name Blue Ruin:
it could go the direction of an old-time moonshine operation, creating something deliciously potent on some floodplain island back in the
days of prohibition; heck, it may well go further back than that, a small
group of people brewing some concoction out on a floodplain island,
their activity out of sight and out of mind of those in the nearby town.
Imagine that small boat, making its way across the side channel with
some effort and with not much freeboard, so heavily is it laden with the
potent brew. Then the distiller making way toward the town, and the
network of buyers awaiting. This isn't such a far-fetched idea, really; all
the same, it may just be a rebellious idea applied to a place that didn't
previously have a name.

As a matter of fact, public lands along the river have been used for
the creation of cultivated products. It has been a well-known fact that,
in places, the Greenway lands have been used to cultivate marijuana in
the past few decades—though it is also likely such grow operations were
pretty small, and few and far between. Up until relatively recently, in the
summer months law enforcement agencies conducted aerial surveys of
the Greenway properties to seek out possible illegal cultivation. In my
many years traveling and walking through a lot of Greenway properties,

I'd never seen such cultivation on Greenway property until, ironically, 2018. By that time marijuana cultivation was legal in Oregon.

Blue Ruin also reminds us of the snowfields high in the Cascade Range, and the blue of the ice that eventually gives way to spring sending its water down into the high-elevation tributaries. Pure water also finds its way into deep fissures in the basalt of the Cascades, forming vast underground sources of cold pristine water from both snow and rain that erupt out of the earth in the form of very pure springs.

From the dancing waters of high tributaries to the creeks that nourish and create rivers, such places should be revered and not taken for granted. In some ways the notion of protecting these waters diminishes as the river grows in size from south to north, with the corresponding growth and impact from towns, farms, and industry. As these waters travel downstream mile after mile, the purity and clarity that appeared at the headwaters degrades. This is certainly true of the Willamette system and is something that can be easily seen by the layperson. This reality reflects a ruinous relationship with rivers, with the efforts to protect water quality failing on multiple fronts. It is easy to find examples of how we give away our water quality based on tradition.

I can recall an Oregon DEQ employee writing me, as recently as 2015, saying that the blackish mass of wastewater covering nearly half the river's width just a mile downstream of a fantastic Greenway site was legal under the Clean Water Act—well, Oregon's interpretation of it. He also tried to tell me that just because it was visible from the air didn't mean it was breaking water quality regulations. Of course, his argument was inaccurate, to say the least.

At question was fourteen million gallons a day of treated wastewater from a pulp mill near Halsey, Oregon, that was being discharged into the Willamette. The dark color of the waste is caused by tannins and other dark by-products from their pulp-making process. From the river, whether you were paddling a canoe or fishing, you could see the discharge from a series of pipes underwater and smell the decaying material. It was the smell of rot.

The discharge covered far too wide an area in the river, beyond what the company's permit allowed. The DEQ tried to make the case that, because a gravel bar had grown upstream, the permit holder wasn't subject to the original requirements of the permit. When I heard this I had to wonder who was minding the store, so to speak, at the Oregon DEQ. In their view it was OK to illegally discharge millions of gallons of effluent into the upper stretch of the Willamette River, as long as the mill was working to correct the problem. Unfortunately, for a series of years the mill had been "working to correct the problem," and even so, it had come to this. It was also interesting given the growing public concern about the variety of pollutants being constantly injected into our world via water and air.

The Oregon DEQ has not reflected what might be termed "the best of the best," over the past thirty years. Don't get me wrong, there are some very good smart people working at the DEQ who are doing good work to curb pollution in Oregon. In fact, some of the new faces at the agency are making some significant changes—and that is a good sign.

The problem historically is that the DEQ is an institution built on cozy relationships with some long-operating industries in the state, industries that also tend to have robust representation in the state legislature, backed by funding for lobbyists and campaign contributions. The same legislature controls the DEQ budget. "Old school," perhaps, describes a legislature accustomed to accommodating the ways of a declining industry along the Willamette (however unsustainably, in this case); too often, established relationships and the money behind them have historically won the day. Logging interests in Oregon also provide a good example of old ties that still exist, even within an industry that has declined because of less cutting on public lands over the past two decades and private lands being managed to cut smaller and smaller trees. Today, private "forest lands" are no longer legitimate healthy forests composed of multiple species and ages. Instead, they are typically monocultures, devoid of the necessary genetic diversity and range of species that natural forests contain. Further, such forests, found along many Willamette River tributaries such as the Calapooia, are harvested in large clear-cuts that leave the watershed in ruins.

This is no big secret. Frankly, anyone with a cursory understanding of state government can describe what constitutes power in relation to government. It seems to me that some of the power behind this old way of doing business has eroded, but it still persists, to the point where the Oregon DEQ is stretched very thin. Hopefully we will see a new trend with increased capacity in the coming years—but when legislators have

professional lobbyists bending their ears seemingly every day that the legislature is in session, with money flowing down different campaign paths,
some of that old power still clings on. It certainly has had an impact over
enforcement of standards, and of holding the line on a variety of situations
that affect clean water, air, and land. Many folks believe that standards
for pollution are too lenient in Oregon and have been on such a path
for a long time. Whether one looks at the use of pesticides, which have
relatively little regulation in comparison to their potential impact, or at
development standards and enforcement, the Willamette and its tributaries bear the burden.

But thankfully, not all is in ruins along the Willamette. Blue Ruin
"island" is a place replete with much of what the Willamette Greenway
natural lands can offer. If you've ever just looked at the rocks along any
river, what you see can be simply amazing: the combination and intermin-
gling of geology interfacing with the long process of erosion, all coupled
with chemistry. It seems all the ingredients are rounded into one, yet dispersed and singular at the same time. Rippling waves of rock can be seen
in the spring after the high flows have diminished, leaving freshly turned
and churned orbs of material ejected and created from volcanic eruptions
and then sculpted and shaped by endless years of water. Looking along
this beach of rounded gray rock, it is a smooth uniformity—each stone
uniquely sculpted and, at the same time, all by the energy of the same
long-practiced natural sculptor. With a warm glow from the afternoon
sun, the waves of rock that emanate from the high silty brown flow are a
stark contrast to the fast springwater. The scene is pure beauty.

Winding like a snake from the main flow of the Willamette, a side
channel extends from the river from about November to June, with the
level of the river enabling enough flow to create a weaving westward
snake-like link. Rounded river rock, like giant mono-colored ostrich eggs,
are everywhere shifted and pushed by the river's current. Vibrant green
willows cling to the sandy, rocky soil, extending their roots into the water
table just a scant few inches below.

Over the years I've stopped at such sites many times, walking up to
where the newly emerged green leaves stretch toward the sunlight. In
some ways the gravel bar island itself is akin to these plants. Shaped each
year to some degree, and newly revealed, the island grows in its own way
and doesn't seem so different from the willows above.

A distinctive dark plume of wastewater is injected into the shallow river water at Halsey, Oregon.

In a slight breeze the willows shimmer, moving as if on their own power. A Pacific willow or a sandbar willow, a Scouler's willow or other species—all of them call some part of the river home. Along the Willamette are a handful of willow species, but at times they can be tricky to identify. The larger tree-sized Pacific willow can have its cousin sandbar willow stretching across a whole gravel bar just upstream. If you go upland just a little bit, the Scouler's willow might be found in patches among the red osier dogwood and ninebark. As you travel inland on the more established floodplain habitats, the matrix of species becomes more complex.

As a paddler moves toward the island on a summer day, with the drop of the river flows, the band of green is at times forty yards from the shoreline. In front of it is a mass of river rock, a great majority of it from two to four inches in diameter. It extends in a rounded, scattered, and seemingly patterned line for a great distance. If you lay on the gravel bar and close one eye and look outward, the rounded expanse is a work of art. It extends like a playa flat, radiating outward in what feels to be an endless swath of gray, rounded, individual artistic elements. A big gravel bar like the one at Blue Ruin has the feel of a panoramic photograph.

One of the main things I noticed at Blue Ruin years ago was hyporheic flow. This kind of flow of water occurs underground, or at least under layers of river rock. You see, large gravel islands and similar landforms can receive the flow of water from upstream and slow it down. In some cases, this flow percolates along, just under the surface of the gravel and soil of the island, then emerges downstream. This notion may be pretty intuitive, given that water can flow through rock, sand, and sediment. What makes this process more noteworthy is that, because of the time spent being filtered, and away from the warmth of the atmosphere and sun—the water emerges typically cooler than the surrounding river water. This makes for a valuable contribution to water quality where it remerges into the current—assuming it has been under the rocks for enough time.

After I had worked about a year on the river, I camped at Blue Ruin for a night. On the fine afternoon I arrived, I had pulled my canoe onshore, made my camp, and was relaxing, walking along the shoreline. At one point I noticed the faint flutter of current spilling from the river rock along the shore and into the back channel. It was a distinct flow I was seeing emerge from the rock. Just above the side channel's surface, water flowed from the rocky shore like a tiny creek emanating from the ground. I bent toward it and touched the water. Since I was standing in the shallow water of the channel, I noticed the distinct difference in temperature. The water gently bubbling from the gravel was perhaps a couple of degrees cooler than the river, maybe more.

Now, the same thing can happen with groundwater from riverside upland areas along the river, with the same cooling affect. Groundwater, moving deep in porous soils, shielded from the sun, is often distinctly cooler than surface water. Hyporheic flows work the same way, but can be a bit more transitory, and found at shallower depths. Generally, hyporheic zones are areas where water travels underground for some distance, fed by a river or stream. Over time the water may cool down, and where the flow reenters a river or stream, it can be cooler than it was when it entered the subsurface area. Along many rivers, gravel bars offer the best visible exemplars of this process.

A large gravel bar can often hold on to water from upstream just long enough to cool it a bit before it flows out of the bar and back into the

Camping along gravels bars like this one can be very peaceful and enjoyable.

river. The Willamette is replete with examples of this kind of cooling flow. That big gravel bar island, about a mile in length, received the water from the river upstream, likely from a variety of elevations, slowed it down in its dense cobble of rounded river rock, sand, and silt, shielding it from the sun just long enough to cool it down a bit. Like a lot of things in life, after you've seen and understood something once, it becomes easier to recognize afterward. On most every subsequent trip along the river, I could not help but look for these seeps, large and small. Sometimes you may not see them but can feel them, as you walk along the shoreline and a distinct coolness covers the sandaled foot.

Blue Ruin is a place to linger. While the City of Eugene is close at hand, it is far enough downriver to gain Blue Ruin a bit of solitude. This place also demonstrates how the river can change the shape of its channel, and the shape of the land around it. Having traveled to this place more than once a year for more than twenty years, I've seen the island carved away on one side, with a new channel emerging down the middle. Pieces of the back channel have been eroded away, while the length of this island seems to have grown. Traveling to it with my daughters and friends always involves just a bit of anticipation as to what the place will look like, if I haven't been there in a while. Notions like this are pretty common to river travel, it seems.

Recently, after a major April flood on the Willamette, I traveled to this island with James T., just a week after the massive flow of muddy water. James and I have traveled the Willamette a lot, usually by canoe. We've rock-hounded, investigated, and cut trails on much of the river When you find people who have that river passion and are smart, good humored, and willing to endure the elements, it makes sense to get those river days on the calendar.

Amazingly, the island appeared roughly as it normally does. We walked a bit inland, then downstream. What I noticed right off, and not due to the flood, was that the fringe of willows along the shoreline was discernibly thicker than it had been just a couple of years before—a good sign for the river. We had to work our way through them to reach a bit of open space beyond. After a few minutes, we found that the beleaguered river register, where people can write about their river travel, was still standing. It was bent to the side and had obviously been under the big flow, but when we opened it, the waterproof notebook and a couple of pens were still there. As usual, I had to take a look at the entries. Some of them were quite humorous. The point of the register was to enable river travelers to indicate where they had put-in along the river, what kind of craft they were traveling in, what their intended destination was, and any other thoughts they had. The "comments" section was always fun, reflecting the good-natured reality of most river travelers. "Great spot, with tons of agates," read one entry. "Longest Day of the Year, and cannot think of a better place to enjoy the river," read another from the previous summer. Such entries went on and on. "Mergansers, swainson's thrushes, quail, bald eagle, merlin, and sapsuckers, this place is awesome!" Another said, "we love this river and will most certainly come back to this island."

I could not agree more. It is hard to imagine not having these public properties to visit along the Willamette.

4
Welcome Solitude

> I can look at the same map day after day, the same square of country,
> and continue to find new things of interest.
> —Alan Kesselheim, *Water and Sky: Reflections of a Northern Year*

Some of the riverlands along the Willamette seem to have their own gravity, a kind of natural draw that makes you want to be there. One such area is called Harkens Lake. Rich and green in the spring, the parcel is gorgeous and dense with floodplain forest. From the river in summer, you see a massive wall of trees that back a wide gravel bar, with the opposite side of the gravel bar, at the river's edge, held close by willow. Behind this peninsula is a long backwater that is rich with life.

Over the years I've been to Harkens Lake often enough that I've lost track of how many times that might be—many, many, many times, at least. It is one of those properties where I'm inclined to just take a moment to enjoy the view and relative quiet—to listen to the Swainson's thrush calling from the forest edge in summer as I was about to paddle by but decided to stop anyway. In winter, to take a quick break to sip a bit of coffee and witness a varied thrush in the winter lowlands. To scan for red-tailed hawks, and bald eagle during any month, is a riverine relief if you take a few minutes in this place.

Engaging with this property from the river, the gravel bar is the main stopping point. In most months it is about a third of a mile in length along the mainstem river's west side (river left). This expanse of rock seems to hold all the colors, sizes, and textures, and many of the fragments of river geology that the Willamette offers. Over the years many people have sought this place to camp, explore, and relax. From my time here, I think it is one of the quietest areas—usually beyond the reach of noise from cars somewhere across the vast agricultural plain to both the west and east, and with little white noise from nearby agricultural properties.

On the east side it is especially vast—just beyond the fringe of trees that line the top of the high bank, a wide expanse with only the occasional sound of machinery to dull the peace. Time here is seldom hindered by the groan of a tractor in a nearby field or encumbered by the whirr of irrigation equipment, which can turn a beautiful place where you may wish to spend the night into an annoying experience that sends most river travelers quickly downstream.

Sound is an issue in our world. In our cities, cars and trucks of all sorts are the dominant feature that make up the daily waves of sound that permeate areas far from the source. At times it all becomes a bit much. Endless successions of noise—from a loud car on a distant road to the rumble of traffic of a nearby interstate—over time this ever-present sound deluge can rob our surroundings of any sense of peace. Noise pollution is a reality that is too seldom addressed, wherever one may be. For many, including me, this barrage makes visits to nature that much more important. To leave behind the typical wall of sound that is the backdrop to many of our lives is a chief attraction of a sojourn into the natural world of the river, from a brief escape to an extended visit. To be surrounded by the sense of peace and the workings of the natural world is part of the allure. Too little thought has been put toward where certain machinery and activity should be allowed, and noise should be better addressed moving forward. Overall though, many places are relatively quiet and peaceful, where one can find birdsong as the dominant sound even in the heart of a well-populated valley. Ironically, even though this river is now being highlighted for low-impact, peaceful recreation, there are some rural areas where the drone of irrigation equipment, gravel quarries, or nearby agricultural machines makes a visit not all that enjoyable for anything other than a short walk. Of course, the American fixation with automobiles frequently results in the worst of the layers of noise that can diminish efforts to find a bit of peace along the river. Thankfully Harkens has little of this.

At the border of the gravel bar and floodplain forest, inset from the river about fifty meters, a dense stand of Oregon ash, cottonwood, ninebark, serviceberry, and more spread to the west. This green swath contrasts with the predominant gray rock of the gravel bar, excluding the willows, of course. If you look carefully, you'll find pathways through the trees and brush made by wildlife, into the forest beyond.

On one visit, I made my way into the forest, listening to the birds of early May. Hummocky, and dense with foliage, the place was alive with the sound of neotropical migrants, and here and there Townsend's warblers, ruby-crowned kinglets, and year-round species such as white-crowned sparrows and towhees flew across the occasional open area. On this trip my eyes found a wildlife camera—likely from a local hunter seeking deer. Of course, placing such cameras on Oregon Parks Greenway properties is illegal. In a few moments, the camera was dismounted.

Wide open, and contoured from high river flows, the gravel bar holds its own seasonal display, seen principally through the lush line of willows that became established a few years back. A few small wispy shoots first seen in 2002 had erupted into a long, thick line of green, matching the shape of the arc of nearly the whole gravel bar. Pacific willow, Scouler's willow, and others thrive there now.

A recent trip to this place held the image for me—with my mind playing on the obvious metaphors of change. Every winter this big bar is flooded, sometimes with a foot or two of water and sometimes with much more. The willow branches are aqua bound, covered with brown silty water. At their base, where the little stalks push into the rounded river rock and micro-grained silt of the river, the rocks hold fast—with some rolling a bit down the bar, and others seemingly anchored against the high water—especially where the willow roots cradle them.

I looked upstream at the gravel bar on this recent trip on an early spring day. After months of dark gray skies, cold weather, and big river flows, all the cottonwood trees seemed about to burst with green. Little green leaves were edging their way out into the world, seizing the faint sun that was growing daily in strength. On that day, frail spring sunlight seemed to be pulling the tender shoots out into the cool air—nanometer by nanometer. In some ways, that shoulder season along the river is a thing to marvel at.

I found myself enjoying a few minutes of sunshine, even pulling a little camp chair out of my canoe to sit on the beach with legs extended to the southwest, facing toward the warmish light. It was a good few minutes. That is how it goes along rivers in northwest Oregon. One has to take it when it is present, with a mind toward being present in those moments. Just a bit later, the low gray clouds made their way across the Coast Range, and soon showered the Willamette floodplain with rain once again.

That day the river was a bit high, about 12,000 cubic feet per second (cfs) at the Harrisburg gauge. To say the least, the river was full of energy, with deep swirling water pulsing northward. Once in a while, full trees could be seen floating by, with their recently exposed tangled masses of interweaving roots dipping into both air and water. A wavy mix of flexible wood, the roots wove into a bundle, holding soil and rocks between them—even as long trunks and root wads floated down the river. Sometimes the whole tree would shiver as it shifted in the current, rattling the long trunk in a quick vibration, shaking the whole length of tree as it quivered against the current. Thousands and thousands of pounds of mass moved easily by the flow.

In non-winter flows, the gravel bar at Harkens is wide and open. Rounded gray rocks expand outward from the floodplain forest, interspersed with patches of sand, both large and miniscule kernels generated and transported across the floodplain landscape. Sometimes the sand surprised me. At the coast, along the dynamic ocean, sand is one thing. Here along this silty, nutrient-rich river, it feels like something transported from another river, or another part of the world, depending on where you find it. Don't get me wrong, fine-grained sand is much welcomed.

I had first camped at Harkens around 2003 with a group of people on an April weekend that had the elements of winter still in tow. At the time, it felt unseasonably cold. Our collection of colorful tents dotted the gravel bar and provided a vivid contrast to the sparse emerging green shoots, with the major backdrop of gray river rock. A bright yellow dome here, the arc of a red rainfly there, and another bright blue synthetic layer of protection against the elements—the precisely cut material decorated the beach. That night the sparks from our campfire rose into the cold and clear night sky as we shared our stories and laughter, all the while watching the stars. By morning, bits of ice spread across the thin bright layers of our tents and other gear. To all of us, the last filaments of winter were a surprise, but one that was welcomed. While our camp tables and kitchen were under a cover, any other gear left on the gravel beach was coated with ice crystals. Soon our campfire was reignited into a morning blaze as people slowly made their way out of the sleeping bags into the frosty morning. Zombie-like movements eroded away as they took in their share of coffee, tea, or anything else hot to drink. It ended up being a banner blue sky morning, something we all appreciated as we prepared for the day.

That river trip was made up of a great group of people. Chief among them was the late John Cooney, who produced the wonderful nature series, *The Natural World*, on the NPR affiliate KLCC in Eugene. John was wonderfully educated in a great many subjects, the world of nature being a central passion. He seemed to add to his knowledge regularly with his forays to mountainsides, wetlands, and of course rivers. He was also a lover of books—and collected them regularly. He and his wife Angela had joined as volunteers on this trip. John had produced a couple bottles of wine the night before. His expertise in the world of the grape vine was well-honed, similar to his study of nature, from many years of research and work in the wine industry. It was just one more reason that it was great to have John around.

On this trip Mr. Cooney had his birding hat on and went to work identifying the early migrating songbirds that were making their way through the riverside forest. He was a keen birder, and always seemed to find joy and a sense of surprise as he identified the spring arrivals whisking amid the riverside forest. I was amazed as he zeroed in on a range of species, from the early arrivals to the resident raptors. Alert, knowledgeable, and eager to allow people to encounter aspects of the natural world that they may not have known much about, John educated us all as he held a steady eye and ear on the riverscape around us, lifting his binoculars to the emerging leaves and listening to and identifying the birdcalls.

Our group took its time breaking camp that morning, as the sun peeked through the trees across the river. Coffee and fire held us glued to the camp. That morning, John and Angela took a walk, making their way through the dense forest vegetation that backed the gravel bar on which we camped. If you found a narrow game trail, chances were that you could find your way through the thick brush, carefully making your way through the occasional naturally barbed blackberry shoots that can so easily complicate the travel of those without a cutting tool.

Behind the initial thick layer of brush and trees, the forest opened up, with the spacing between the ash, willow, and cottonwood becoming wider. Here the ground is shaped in parallel depressions that extend for dozens of meters—small temporary channels molded by the high flows of winter. In many floodplain forests you find similar elements of the floodplain soils being sculpted by the water. Behind the immediate curtain of trees, a narrow meadow let the spring sunlight filter through, enough to show a more open forest just to the west. Walking in for a few minutes and making your way westward, the openness of the back water can be seen. By Willamette terms, this property is expansive and provides a wealth of high-quality habitat.

After a while John and Angela could be seen emerging from the narrow trail through the willows. John had an amused look on his face. "How was your walk," I asked. John smiled, "We just saw a Roosevelt elk, parked over here in the forest—a big bull," John said, pointing into the tangle of trees. The two of them had carefully made their way along a deer path, keeping quiet to listen to and see the birds, which turned out to be an excellent strategy for witnessing other wildlife that might be present in the floodplain. Instead of birds, as they moved to the west through the forest toward the old dead-end back channel, there stood the elk.

Our group was bemused and excited to hear this news, with "That is so cool" being the common response to John and Angela's sighting. Deer were persistently abundant along the river at times, and we could see them all along the Willamette, though we still loved to witness their ways along the river. Yet Roosevelt elk upped the ante in the fragmented floodplain forest. Elk are relatively large compared to black-tailed deer, and to know that there were elk moving about within sight of the river put a smile on my face. In the macroscale, it was potentially good to know that elk were capable of moving from larger protected areas to riverside greenways.

The Finley National Wildlife Refuge is just a few miles to the west of Harkens, and it is conceivable this animal had made its way across the highway, then across a couple of rural roads and multiple farm fields to make its way to Harkens. It may have been complete happenstance for this animal, but it was there. Or perhaps this was a really smart elk who, having learned the ropes years ago, knew that in early spring it could find what it needed along the river. Either way, when I think of John and Angela at that time, it seems to me that their smiles told enough. It was there, and that was the only fact that mattered.

Since that time, it has become clear to me that elk use the Greenway at least somewhat regularly. A few sightings occur each year. I was surprised not long ago to have a friend text me a photo of a small herd of elk making their way across the farm fields and small stands of trees near the river in Linn County, then likely dipping into the large Greenway at Sam

Daws Landing, just a few miles downstream of Harkens. In thinking about the need for healthy habitat along the river, what holds true for salmon—needing to have healthy natural areas at regular intervals along the river at a minimum—the same holds true for elk, birds, and other species that have large home ranges. One might consider this to be a strong argument for establishing additional Greenway natural areas along the river.

It is fitting that John and Angela spotted the lone floodplain elk on that day. I had just met John a short time prior to that trip and had had the pleasure of spending time with him on two other river trips, as well as some larger work-related events. He would serve on the board of my organization for several years. One wonderful memory is having a beer with him and another colleague after we had had a major conservation success on the upper Willamette at Norwood Island, about twelve years after the Harkens trip. Just a few months after that celebratory brew, I received a voicemail from John saying I should call him. I called back immediately, and he informed me he had cancer that had spread from his stomach to his brain. He had felt fine, but just a few days before, he had wavered in the kitchen. Angela got him to the hospital, where they suspected he had had a minor stroke. Further tests revealed the reality.

Just a few weeks later, he passed away. At his funeral a friend quoted John as saying, "This is the best death ever," given the many friends who had come to his side to spend time until his final hours. The many people around him as he fought cancer was an extraordinary testament to the person he was. After his passing I went back to the KLCC website and listened to many of his *Natural World* pieces, many that I had never heard before. I listened to his last entry—at the Snag Boat Bend Unit of the Finley Wildlife Refuge, along the Willamette River—several times at least. He was a natural storyteller, with an inquisitive mind that gathered in facts and held on tightly. His deep resonant voice was perfect for radio—he should have had many years more to create radio stories that took one to the natural world, including many other Greenway properties.

Over the years, I've had long discussions with people about the handful of public lands along the Willamette, seeking to advance an expansion of the Greenway program to include more acreage. State budgets willing, we concluded that the state could devote a specific amount to acquiring private lands from willing sellers along the river. In addition to lands being put into conservation easements, and other purchases by nonprofit conservation organizations, the level of public ownership along the river could be increased to the benefit of a more robust river ecosystem, and to benefit recreation. It appears that perhaps a sense of optimism about such actions can be discerned among some people over the last few years — and that in and of itself is a gain for the river, or at least for some of the folks who are working on it.

More recently I had a chance to camp again at Harkens for a couple of nights. It was a July weekend, and we had the big gravel bar to ourselves. My wife Erica and me, two dogs (Merlin and Blade), and tons of wildlife. That weekend a few canoeists and kayakers passed late in the afternoon on both days, but they paddled on to other campsites easily found starting a mile downstream. What frequently punctuated the stillness was the presence of bald eagle.

As you may remember, the bald eagle was taken off the federal Endangered Species List in 2007. For a long period, this bird was poisoned, shot, and had its habitat altered to the point where its numbers were greatly reduced from historic norms. At one point in the early 2000s, bald eagle poisonings were occurring in Linn County. Clearly a person was set on killing some of these birds for some reason. An intensive public education effort, with law enforcement, seemed to work, as the occurrences diminished. It is hard to believe that someone would do that, even if eagles prey on the occasional young farm animal. Such actions are one of the key reasons the Endangered Species Act exists. After many years of protection and recovery efforts to rebuild the population, the endangered status was lifted. Along the Willamette River, there is a seemingly healthy population, and in fact, statewide, the population is large and growing.

Time and again as we sat on the river's edge, sipping a beverage and reading books, we heard the high-pitched call of adult eagles, soon followed by the subadults. Adult bald eagles have the distinct white head and tail feathers; juvenile birds maintain their dark plumage typically until about their fifth year. Sometimes the observer can confuse a juvenile bald eagle with an adult golden eagle — both being dark-brownish and flecked with a range of lighter-colored feathers. While the golden eagle population is larger than that of the bald eagle in Oregon, most of its population is located east of the Cascade Range. From time to time, golden eagles are identified in the Willamette Valley, and they are wonderful to spot.

What may be less known is that the population of bald eagles along the Willamette is extraordinary.

What we witnessed that weekend was likely the adults and their juveniles that were reared in a nearby nest. On and off the communication went for hours between these birds. In an ongoing cycle, the great birds would alight on the fir trees at the river's edge, on the far bank, then would take off abruptly—urged by some unknown sense to launch and circle the floodplain lands. Sometimes these birds would stay for twenty minutes in one place, clinging with their talons to the high dark fir branches, giving us a great view through the spotting scope. Off to the east of Harkens, unseen by us on the other side or the river at the water's edge, is a vast agricultural field. The birds were alighting on what is only a thin fringe of trees separating the vast field from the river. When I looked later at some aerial photographs, it was easy to wonder what kinds of chemicals may be regularly applied to that field, and how much of the runoff from that vast altered landscape makes its way into the river, and into the eagles? Ahh, the mind of a person who understands how toxic pollutants can work can be haunting.

It may be that the display of eagle vitality we viewed that day was enhanced by the assemblage of natural lands at Harkens. In what at times seemed like continuous motion paired with the high-pitched vocalizations of these birds, the eagles continued their flying and landing on the riparian trees pretty consistently for our two days there, shifting a bit upstream and then downstream, but all on the same mile stretch. Here I feel the need to mention that the bald eagle has a high, at times squeaky, and typically intermittent call. One might even say the call is a bit shrill. Contrasting greatly is the call of the red-tailed hawk that has been ever so frequently used by mistake for the call of the bald eagle in film and video. As most any person with a bit of bird knowledge can tell you, this ongoing gaff from a variety of film and television artists goes back decades.

In our time at Harkens, the eagles climbed and rode the summer thermals to great heights, and at other times they would fly in pairs, whisking along the top of the cottonwoods, then disappearing around the bend.

While the recovery of the bald eagle is generally an Endangered Species Act success story, a great many species of plants and animals along the Willamette have been introduced, with some of them causing great harm and others posing potential threats. As we sat there along the water's edge, resting our feet in the cool water, we noticed a bright red creature moving along the river bottom just a few feet from where we sat. It was in the shallows, about five feet out. "What is that?" I asked aloud, but as soon as I uttered the words, it was evident what the object was—a crayfish.

Almost immediately I recognized this bright, red-shelled creature. This species was not from the Willamette system. Heck, it was not a species native to Oregon. This was a red swamp crayfish (*Procambarus clarkii*). As the name implies, the color of this rather large crayfish is often bright red, sometimes a more muted red. The length of this one was about eight inches, and its pincers were a couple inches long. We watched it as it approached. It carried itself along with what felt like a sense of acute awareness of us, as it pointed its dark, protruding little eyes our way.

As a boy I used to go to our neighborhood creek with friends after school and on weekends and summer breaks. Looking back, it seems we were at that little suburban creek in Milwaukie, Oregon, a lot. Some of that time had to do with fantastic "expeditions," wherein we would walk along the creek, an activity more commonly known to us as "creek walkin." Some of these journeys were to search out tadpoles and salamanders. We'd pass through culverts under the local roads, testing our mettle. Other times found us carefully lifting up rocks to catch the abundant crayfish. Sometimes the local park was the goal, and given that we had to pass by the backyards of many suburban houses on such journeys, there was a sense of accomplishment when we'd reach our goal. Avoiding barking dogs, dumped yard debris, junk protruding through a wooden fence, or the occasional adult who might spy our path—reaching the park was an achievement! Much of the creek was lined with rock and weeds. Back then I had no idea what an invasive weed was, nor did I care. Instead, like my friends, it was about pickling our sneakers in creek water that at times was of questionable cleanliness.

Many times, on these spring afternoons or long summer days, we'd encounter a variety of flows and marvel at the color of the water, or even witness an occasional sheen. Even back in the 1970s as a kid, before the advent of today's more comprehensive environmental education in many schools, we knew the sheens were not a good find for people, or for the crayfish that lived in the creek. Understanding pollution was pretty intuitive. At that age we'd seen documentaries and depictions of pollution of multiple types. For me it may well have been Bill Mason's book and film,

Paddle to the Sea, and others in that vein, that brought the images of pollution to the fore, underscoring that sullied water, land, and air were things to prevent. Though the materials varied in form and approach, to me it feels like the teachers I had in elementary school in the 1970s did a good job of communicating some essential facts.

Instinctively as kids we had a feel for the transition of this creek through the neighborhoods and eventually to the Willamette River, about a mile downstream. We knew the houses, the rocky shoreline in places, the sheens and the occasional junk and garbage were not *of the creek*. Raised as a kid of the bottle bill, like many others we'd search high and low for the detritus of the unthinking person, seeking out the many cans and bottles found along the creek in places and nearby roadsides. It kept us busy, and kept us moving upstream and down.

Of course, it can be argued that our impact on the small creatures of the creek was not a wondrous contribution to biodiversity—many times we'd carry our prey home in glass jars. Myriad tadpoles swirling around, trapped in the murky water, with jars set on kitchen tables was a regular occurrence. The poor creatures endured a somewhat wicked journey. Usually after a day or two the aquatic finds would be set free back at the creek. The crayfish were most often sought. The signal crayfish (*Pacifastacus leniusculus*) were the ones populating that small creek, native to the Northwest and seemingly thriving at that time.

Compared to the red swamp crayfish that can be found today, the signal crayfish has more of a brownish tone, though sometimes they would also exhibit a bit of a reddish hue. They also have a white fleck near the joint in their front pincers, making them easier to positively identify. We'd carefully tread along the creek, lifting rocks here and there looking for the quick surge of the crayfish swimming backward in a single evasive rush, their instinctive move to get away from the large forms above the water overhead. We learned to anticipate where we'd find them, and at what flows. As we crouched carefully, being sure not to move a muscle, the little crustaceans would appear next to a rock, and we'd anticipate its movement backward. At other times the pincers would be raised in a defensive posture, the little eyes seeming to project a fierce desire to stay alive and defend itself, if for only one more time.

Once in a while the little creatures would hit their mark, as the hand of a kid sought to reach in from behind and grasp the body with a thumb and forefinger. "Aieee, he got me!" and the little creature would drop through the air and back into the shelter of the water and rock.

As we surveyed the red swamp crayfish at Harkens Lake, making its way upriver, I got up, thinking that perhaps I'd catch this one and end its life. You see, this species of crayfish is invasive, meaning that it does no good for the native signal crayfish, and impacts the health of river habitat. More aggressive than the signal, these reddish little monsters simply outdo the native ones, outcompeting them in their habitat and conflicting with them directly. According to the Oregon Department of Fish and Wildlife, this is a species of concern and is highly invasive. More work should be done to better understand their distribution. Recently I set a series of traps from Salem, then downstream a few miles. The goal was to determine whether any red swamp crayfish could be found along a given stretch of river. In what might be a bit of good news, no red swamp crayfish were caught below Salem. Such work in many areas needs to continue to track their potential spread throughout the Willamette watershed, given how persistent they are and how they negatively impact signal crayfish.

To take the life of a creature that just happens to be tough, resilient, and adaptive in some ways might seem wrong. In people those are traits we are typically taught to respect, traits that allow us to get through tough

An adult signal crayfish moves in the shallows at the river's edge.

times and to deal with adversity. In the case of the red swampers, we instead must maintain the analytical approach.

A while after this trip to Harkens Lake, we were with a large group camping at a property nearby and someone had captured a red swamp crayfish and placed it in a bucket. People had been looking at it and marveling at its defensive position—this animal seemed to eye every person who leaned over to look, with those dark, protruding little beads. In some ways it offered up the sentiment of "Look, I'm tough, I made it and live here. So, leave me alone!" The small creature that had been captured was entrained for a couple of hours in the heat, in just a few inches of water at the bottom of a plastic bucket. I was conflicted by this situation. It was at least inhumane. While I am an ardent believer that invasive species must be controlled if we are to have a fighting chance of saving a healthy and functioning ecosystem along the river, at times it is natural to wonder where the dividing line is between what is realistic and what is an impossible task. This is especially true in the case of the ever-spreading impact of invasive plants and animals, and how to deal with them—or where or whether we should try to deal with them. For that crayfish, though, it may have been a lucky day—perhaps the bucket accidentally got knocked over, or maybe it cut its way through the thick plastic with those big claws. What I do know is that it didn't stay in that bucket for too much longer.

In the floodplain lands along the river that bear some resemblance to healthy floodplain forest, the usual assemblage of trees and shrubs include Pacific, sandbar, Scouler's, and other willows; Oregon ash, red osier or creek dogwood, and black cottonwood; and a swath of shrubs such as snowberry, poison oak, ninebark, and others. Sometimes, though, wild native species crop up that are a complete surprise.

At the lower western edge of the back-channel alcove at Harkens is a small access point for camping from the river. Just behind is an open area of a few acres, then behind that an agricultural field. To the untrained eye, the open area may look to be an unkempt field with tall weeds, perhaps Scotch broom growing every few feet. Yet instead of Scotch broom, this area is replete with an anomalous plant—ceanothus. If you've never seen a ceanothus plant, let alone along the floodplain, with a bit of inspection you'll find they are far different than most anything else in the area. At Harkens Lake the plants are large, many standing about five feet in height. Seeming to stretch and bend like modern dancers contorting

A flowering *ceanothus* along the river.

their bodies, bending up and out in myriad directions, the old ceanothus hold fast there to the grit of the floodplain soil. If you have any sense of plants that love arid regions, ceanothus have that feel. My mind wanders to some high south-facing slope somewhere in the southern Willamette Basin, where I'd be more inclined to expect them.

The leaves are small, oval, waxy, and dark green—about half the size of your fingernail. Their branches weave about, though there is a sparse aspect. Brown and gnarled, the branches reach upward, here and there with the little shiny leaves, and in the spring a wonderful finely laced white flower emerges, usually about an inch and a half in diameter. Walking across the open area, one finds dozens of these plants that are otherwise seldom seen in the floodplain. Here, the gnarled specimens almost seem to be *old-growth* ceanothus.

Along the Willamette floodplain, these plants are very few and far between. Saying that there are a handful of sites would be an exaggeration. Ceanothus exist along the Willamette, with care and isolation. What makes the collection at Harkens so unusual is that there are more than fifty plants in this one area. Most other occurrences along the river have only several. At this site, the soil dictates a lot. It is very well drained, dry, and full of small rock delivered by the river. It is crusty and dry after the spring rains stop. As well drained as the site is, even though it is inundated by floods fairly often, the ceanothus are seemingly treated to just the right conditions to enable them to thrive.

Walking this site over the years, trying to stop here in the spring when the flowers are blooming, it is easy to wonder how this group of plants established here. Did someone plant them? Did floodwaters carry just the right amount of seeds downstream, landing at this site under the ideal conditions a couple decades back? Ceanothus seeds seem tough and are easy to see after the flowers have lapsed, with the seeds concentrated in a tight collection of brown minuscule nuggets at the top. Each hard, round little seed sits on a cup, and the cup is connected to the stem. Frequently by mid-July this assemblage has dried out, and the seeds have fallen to the ground around the plant, though the timing can vary by plant.

Over the past few years, I've encountered other sites with a ceanothus or two, and I've also discovered areas where the plant is not established but the soil conditions seem to be ideal. On more than one occasion I've made a small seed collection and carried a few of them to other sites, planting them carefully in the thin, highly drained soils. As of yet, I've seen no sprouts—but you never know what might occur somewhere down the line.

5
A River Treasure

Civilization after civilization has risen on the strength of its natural resources and then fallen as the resources were abused and exhausted.
— Chris Maser, *The Redesigned Forest*

Bleached out and hot to the touch, the rocks along the shoreline of the river were desiccated after long weeks in the heat of summer. Algae had grown along the shoreline when the water was higher back in July, but now in late August the vibrant green, reminiscent of swamp creature slime of 1950s Hollywood, had transformed to a white crust-like coating as the water levels dropped and left the shoreline baking in the sun. For a few days the natural algal green may have withstood the push of the heat, leaving a slimy expanse at the water's edge, but that didn't last long in the onslaught of the direct summer sun in the following days.

Here and there along the river's edge, irregular shapes broke the pattern. Instead of the ovals of dried algae-covered rocks, pieces of wood mixed into the riverside assemblage, a normal sight in most riverside areas. Sometimes the wood mixed with plastic bits, or a carelessly lost soda bottle, or perhaps a straw—items too often found in rivers around the world. Yet, among these signs of human presence, the natural world poked through with other offerings; here and there amid the rock and wood, fragments of something else could be seen: black in places, then off-white, they appeared as thin fragments. Upon closer inspection, some were broken in half, while some were nearly whole, and as big as some of the rocks. After a moment, as I scanned a small length of shoreline, it was clear that I was seeing shells. Though some had clearly been along the riverside for a while and had endured the same summer-baked fate as the river rock, the shells were generally black.

It was a hot afternoon in the late summer of 2001, and I'd been canoeing for a few hours when I stopped for lunch on a large Greenway property known as Sam Daws Landing. Although I had a background in the natural world, with some depth, from fish and birds to the wildflowers and ungulates roaming our natural lands and waters, paired with training in environmental science, I was certainly no expert in every single species along the Willamette, and the large dark shells were a mystery to me.

I knew that the small, sometimes numerous clam species, with abundant shells here and there along the shoreline about an inch in length, were named *Corbicula*. The little clams were not native to the Willamette and were seemingly on the road to being classified as invasive. Here and there were patches of a small native snail species in the genus *Juga*, with several species native to the Pacific Northwest. The little juga snails have dark swirled cone-shaped shells, and they cling with what seems like tenacity to the rocks in the near-shore area. Juga generally indicate decent if not good water quality, and their little black shells are a wonder to look at. But in the case of the larger black shells, I was drawing a blank. Mussel-like, these larger shells reflected a species of something else entirely. They reminded me of razor clam shells, or saltwater mussels: about five to six inches in length, in the shape of an elongated oval, their remnants could be seen at intervals along this beach.

I picked up a specimen; it had two halves (valves), with the formerly stretchy sinew of the now-dried hinge barely keeping the two halves together in their dried-out state. The two halves were open about a centimeter. It seemed the deceased creature had been out in the sun for quite a while, with a smear of river silt and bits of dried algae clinging to the shell. I gently pulled on the shell, working to open it farther. After a few seconds the two halves were laid out.

Inside, the shell had a whitish pearl-like interior, seemingly painted with a glossy but faint hue of pink. Feeling the surface with my finger, it was smooth. It seemed the creature had not been dead all that long. On the outside, the shells were a flat black. The outer layer of the shell was chipped away here and there, with some of the black finish flaking off in places. The living tissue of the organism had been eaten or rotted away, but the smell of the dead animal still lingered, and was unmistakable.

I thought back to some reading I'd done a few years prior on a variety of western river species, and something came to mind—this must be some form of freshwater mussel. It was an animal that was pretty new to me, but one I had thought was more associated with rivers of the East Coast, or higher tributaries in the West. Yet as I looked at the shell, I realized that this is what I was holding. Was it normal in this system along the main river? Where did the live ones come from? I had no idea.

Making the obvious next step, or so it seemed at the time, I waded in the nearshore area, scanning the shallows for anything resembling a long oval shell on the river bottom. I had another hour that I could spend, at least, and of course it was rivertime, so my sense of time as it is generally known was off just a bit anyway. What feels like fifteen minutes on the river can in reality be forty-five minutes, an hour perhaps, or even more. Anyone who has traveled rivers on a regular basis can understand this sense of time being hard to track. Two hours can morph to a half day, and a fifteen-minute walk through a Greenway forest can become a ninety-minute hike with little effort.

It was mid-afternoon, so the light was about as good as it would get. I peered into the shallows, walking carefully among the river rocks and looking beneath the surface. Polarized sunglasses can help the view into the water, and I had mine, which cut the glare from the water's surface. My goal was to view the river bottom in the shallows, from the shoreline to maybe three or four feet out. Mussels are typically nestled into the river bottom, with only part of their shell visible amid the rocks, sediment, and sand.

Each and every footstep in the shallow water was slow, allowing me to look carefully at the river bottom. I felt I was onto something, perhaps a new discovery along the riverine trail I had just started on. Smashing anything with my foot, especially a freshwater mussel, was not what I wanted to do as I stepped across the river bottom with care; every sandaled advance was as careful as I could make it. After an hour or so of seeing nothing but small native fish, I had to get back into the canoe and be on my way. Mussels were somewhere in the river near here, but they sure weren't adjacent to the shells on the shoreline, from what I could see that day. Into my dry bag the shell specimen went. I paddled out of there with a keen interest in whatever this shell represented, and a desire to learn about it. Sometimes life just hands you something really interesting, even if you don't understand its full meaning at the time. It seems all of us have those kinds of moments of one kind or another, formative situations that you later realize somehow changed your course for the better.

When I returned to my house, I scanned the books I had on river species, but they didn't provide a match. In a rambling effort, walking around my house and garage as I put my gear away, I tried to think of the resources I had at hand to identify what this shell represented. Heck, I had quite a few river-related wildlife books, yet nothing I could think of within those pages might provide the answer. Then I recalled a website I'd seen and recognized the likelihood that something online could point me in the right direction.

Onto my computer I went, and after a bit of searching I found a photo, and the identification was pretty clear—it was a freshwater mussel. After a bit more searching for western species, even with the scant information online back then, I learned the shell in question belonged to the *Margaritifera falcata*, more commonly known as the western pearlshell mussel. Black-and-white photographs depicted the mussel—with someone holding some of the live animals, which provided good scale for the shells I'd seen along the Willamette. That was indeed an opening for me to a species that was seldom heard of in most quarters, even in the river world of the western United States. I was completely surprised to learn that this animal could live to be more than a hundred years old in the right conditions! At the time, and even now, that fact provided an immediate level of respect for this native mollusk.

My mind went into overdrive on the hypothetical images, a freshwater mussel filtering for decades on the river bottom. What a completely amazing notion of survival! Soon a bit of research revealed to me that *Margaritifera* are present in a lot of rivers and creeks in Oregon, and other western states. Indeed, they are present—but not always numerous. They are also very poorly documented. In fact, this native freshwater mussel could be found through much of the state, as well as in Washington, Montana, and beyond. It also became clear that, while they were known of in many places, the data for their overall abundance and known populations were scant for a variety of rivers and streams in Oregon.

Other related native mussel species were present as well in the Willamette system, including the Oregon floater and the western ridged mussel. They were not all that well documented but known to exist, with this being especially true of the western ridged mussel. These filter-feeding animals that could live for many decades are little-known, compared with the native fish species, some of which are coveted by anglers and others receiving federal protection of one sort or another.

One treasure trove of good data has been a retired Oregon Department of Fish and Wildlife biologist named Al Smith. When Al retired from ODFW in the late 1990s, he decided he needed a new area of inquiry to keep him engaged in the river world. Freshwater mussels were just the thing to fill that need. Accounts of mussels over the past twenty years in the Northwest are largely thanks to Al Smith's energy on his own expeditions, and to him becoming an inspiration to others: Al has been a leading force for mussel identification since his retirement, and a leading force in terms of educating other people about mussel species found in the Pacific Northwest. Many of Al's contributions have been captured in the database of Northwest mussels, and Al has continued to volunteer on mussel studies and presence/absence surveys in recent times.

Another standout researcher and leader in mussel work in the Northwest has been Celeste Searles Mazzacano, a PhD entomologist who took a liking to mussels in 2007. Her research and ability to communicate about why mussels are overlooked, and deserving of consideration and protection, has helped elevate the understanding of freshwater mussels in Oregon and beyond. Mazzacano regularly conducts projects for a wide array of organizations and institutions seeking to learn more about mussels, or to move them, in the case of projects that could harm known mussel assemblages in our rivers.

Some studies of freshwater mussels have been done in the Northwest, but the species has played second fiddle to the charismatic native fish, such as salmon, steelhead, cutthroat trout, and others. For decades those species have driven efforts to improve the health of river systems, with mussel species mostly unmentioned.

Freshwater mussels were not a principal food source for the native peoples of the Northwest but were a part of the diet during times of hardship, according to historical accounts. During the cold months, when river flows were high but foods more scarce, freshwater mussels were in known locations and were harvestable, depending on the river's flow. Generally, though, knowledge of the presence of freshwater mussels has been scarce to most people. East of the Rocky Mountains, the abundance of mussel species increases and, as a result, more research has occurred there over time.

An adult western
pearlshell mussel
(*Margaritifera falcata*)
near Norwood Island.

From the time I saw those first shells on the beach, I delved further
into this species and, over the next couple of years, learned a bit more
about the biology and the habitats that typically support them. Not until
the summer of 2003, when I was canoeing down a long side channel on
the Willamette, did I formulate a few key questions that would help guide
my work in future years.

Keeping some of the known locations of mussel beds "unknown" is
a nice idea but, given media coverage in the last few years and groups of
people traveling down the river to look at these species, the proverbial
cat is out of the bag. The Norwood Island side channel I was paddling at
that time fits that mold. There are still places along the Willamette that
are little known or visited, and it seems that is a good thing, especially
given the amount of information flowing at us each and every day about,
seemingly, *everything*. The important notion is that the kind of habitat
depicted in relation to where mussels are found still exists in multiple
places on the Willamette River system. Taking this a bit further, it is likely
that freshwater mussels are present in river stretches up and down the

Willamette watershed. But what is true in my experience is that there is nothing else quite like what is described below.

So, there I was with a colleague of mine in a canoe in early July of 2003, at the Norwood Island side channel. We had been evaluating the quality of the riverside habitat along that particular stretch of side channel, and also focusing on the kind of land use that was common at the river's edge. Side channels can be, by their very nature, unpredictable—clogged with fallen trees or dense brambles left by the high flows of winter. After just a few tens of meters into this one, we had to negotiate a tree that had fallen halfway across the channel, extending about twenty feet into the channel right at the water's surface. A couple of quick paddle strokes maneuvered the canoe through the gap between the dark swath of bark and extending branches to the right and the bank on the left. Then we paddled under the old agricultural bridge that was somehow still standing after getting structurally compromised by the flood of 1996.

As we passed the midpoint of this channel, I happened to glance down into what was maybe three feet of water we were floating on. As I did this, with just the right angle of sunlight, I caught the unmistakable presence of what looked to be mussel shells against a light-colored mix of silt and sand on the river bottom. Dark oval forms could be seen every so often, slightly out of focus, as seen through the lens of river water. Floating above them, we turned the canoe upstream and paddled gently, holding ourselves in place as we looked down into the quickly flowing water. Yep, they weren't just the empty shells seen along the shoreline—many of the shells were closed, with live mussels inside! We could even see the minutiae of the small openings, or apertures, along the slightly opened shells that inhaled water and exhaled filtered water back into the river.

We both marveled at the number of shells we could see dotting the river bottom. As the quick flow of the side channel zipped by us, we worked to hold ourselves in place in the shade of the riverside foliage. A healthy weave of red osier dogwood, willow, and other natives provided the shade—which is something that is ideal on rivers and creeks to help keep the water cool. On the other side of the channel was a large open field, with a thin line of trees buffering the expanse of agricultural land from the water of the river.

We continued downstream, floating as slowly as possible. Suddenly the entire bottom of the channel was black with shells. It wasn't just a few mussels here and there along the bottom, it looked like a massive and dense colony of thousands. The huge bed of western pearlshell mussels was situated on both the rocks and the silt of the river bottom. We both looked down into the water, mystified at what we were seeing. Having traveled much of the river system to that point, and many locations more than once, I had never seen anything like it on the mainstem Willamette.

Guessing at the size of the bed at that time, it was about one canoe length wide by ten canoe lengths long. Sure, such measurement doesn't contain an ounce of official protocol for measurement, nor any standardized measure, but it should give you a sense of what we saw at the time. Of course, the measurement of "rods" is well known in many places for portaging canoes, and a rod is based generally on a canoe length. Perhaps "canoe length" should be put to use more often today—all set against the metric system. At any rate, in previous travels along the river it was more typical to spot, if one was lucky, small collections of relatively few mussels along the shoreline—resembling in no way what we saw on this side channel. What we were looking at was a something pretty unique.

To get a bit of rest from trying to keep the canoe in place, or moving upstream in the current, we made our way to a small gap in the riparian zone, where a silty beach existed, and tied the canoe off to the branches. Standing at the shoreline, we walked carefully into the water, scanning the river bottom. Long and oval, with flecks of white seen amid the black outer layer of the shell, the mussels seemed to be everywhere. There were easily hundreds and hundreds of live mussels every few feet.

All kinds of questions came to mind. Why was this magnificent mussel bed here? How many live animals were there among the mix of dark shells? Of the dark, empty shells, why were they empty, and had they died of natural causes? What conditions in this channel enabled it to support such a large number of these animals? My mind was filled with such questions, all of them framed by the marvel that this animal had had such seeming success living in the river system at all, given their limitations— from scant ability to move away from harm to the fact that these animals were subject to whatever the river, and all of us, sent their way.

Generally speaking, the freshwater mussel has a bivalved shell, with an intake opening and an outlet. Water flows into the animal where it passes through their gills and is filtered. The openings are known as the inhalant and exhalant apertures, which are located on the narrower end of the shell and facing upstream. The other end of the shell is typically inches into the river bottom, which secures the mussel against the current. Enabling the flowing water to make its way into their bodies is how they gain the nutrients they need. On the opposite end of the shell, the end typically inches into the river bottom, is a tough, fleshy protrusion called a "foot." The foot can help the mussel move—slowly, to be sure—and excavate its way into the substrate and even hold onto sediment and rock. I found myself imagining the intake of water that these animals conduct almost continuously, filtering food, other nutrients, and of course pollutants for the full extent of their lives, all the while moving slowly here and there, or into the substrate with its foot.

It seems a pretty amazing feat for any living thing to remain on the river bottom, and to grow in such a way—all the time with a very limited ability to move far from harm. Mussels can move, but very slowly, and typically remain very near where they were juveniles, unless they are swept downstream by strong river flows. And although their ability to survive in such a way is surprising, it is their reproductive cycle that seems to stretch reality.

When mature, the male mussels release sperm into the water, which the nearby females incorporate. The sperm fertilizes the egg in the female, and soon larvae begin to develop in the female. The larvae are called glochidia. At just the right time, the glochidia are released by the female into the water. In what seems the ultimate game of chance, a few of the glochidia find their way into the gills or fins of native fish—in the case of the western pearlshell, the native fish are thought to be salmon, winter steelhead, and, potentially, cutthroat trout. It seems clear the survival of wild spring chinook and winter steelhead, both listed as threatened under the federal Endangered Species Act, in the Willamette River system is essential to sustaining freshwater mussels.

The tiny glochidia then ride around on these fish for a few weeks or even months (again, little research in Oregon documents the specifics of this key period) before maturing into tiny juvenile mussels. At some undetermined moment, perhaps dictated by water flow, water temperature, chemistry, or some other unknown variable, the small mussel detaches from the gills of the fish and floats away. It is not well known exactly what triggers the release from the fish gills—which, in the case of the western pearlshell, is another very intriguing area for potential study.

It has been said that perhaps only one in a million of these tiny glo-chidia released from the female mussel end up surviving into adulthood. Floating in the water, the tiny mussel that detaches from the fish gill sinks back to the river bottom in flowing water and, if lucky, finds its way between the rocks, other mussel shells, and wood and embeds itself in the silt or sand. Here the tiny animal has a chance to grow, beginning what can be a very long life of more than one hundred years. The odds of the small mussel floating down from the gills of the fish to successfully land on the river bottom seems improbable at best.

This is truly an amazing story of reproduction, containing multiple stages, with each one presenting high risk of failure. Just the right condi-tions are necessary to make it to the next stage, with so very much depen-dent on native host fish swimming somewhere nearby. Clearly this cycle is another astounding example of the complexity of life.

In the years since I first learned about this species and what it takes for them to successfully reproduce, my level of respect has only increased. Worldwide, the Southeast United States has an amazing diversity of mus-sel species, with more than a hundred species of mussels in some states. Research into mussels has been led generally from that region as well as the Midwest, with years of efforts to protect and even reintroduce spe-cies where they have been extirpated. The Northwest has only the west-ern pearlshell, western ridged, winged floater, and a couple of species in the genus *Anodonta* (the Oregon floater and the California floater). That being said, the Northwest has a strong and growing contingent of both professionals and enthusiasts who are working on freshwater mus-sel research and conservation. Though the many mussel species east of the Continental Divide display an array of shapes, colors, and sizes, the reproductive cycle of all remains very similar across the board.

Looking at the breadth of mussel species in North America, one sees that mussels have been greatly affected by human activity. Negative impacts include sedimentation from a variety of sources, disruption of habitat from construction of roads and buildings, a wide array of pollution types, altered stream flows from dams, and drought. All these changes have likely spurred the decline of mussels across North America. In addition, early on, some mussel shells were used to make buttons for clothing, which had an effect in the 1800s. Of course, anything affecting the presence or abundance of host fish can have a direct influence as well, from some of the issues listed above, to the presence of dams. The major decline of some species has resulted in some being listed under the federal Endangered Species Act, with efforts to better protect the remaining populations. The past decade has seen additional understanding and effort to protect and restore these amazing species.

One major area of hope has come from efforts to propagate mussel species artificially, and then release juveniles into streams and rivers. In addition to better protecting against human impacts, this area of research holds some promise for restoring mussels to areas where they have been decimated, though any artificial propagation can come with compromises. This work is ongoing now at multiple sites in North America, with some success being seen in propagation and reintroduction. As with anything of this nature, it can be very complicated to get all of the technical elements just right.

In other areas, work to restore host fish has yielded results. Recent work on the spectaclecase mussel in Minnesota has been intriguing. This species has been reduced massively in some areas and especially in the Mississippi, Missouri, and Tennessee Rivers, where it once had a broad reach. Today it is said only a few isolated populations remain, in a large area above a dam.[1] Efforts to reintroduce this mussel were hampered because the host fish for this species was unknown. After much research into which host fish could successfully transport the glochidia of the spectaclecase, in 2017 researchers at the Center for Aquatic Mollusk Programs at the Minnesota Department of Natural Resources identified two small native fish called goldeneye and mooneye as the glochidia hosts for the spectaclecase mussel, also noting that these species were nearly absent above a key dam. The effort took many years of research across a broad array of fish and other species that could be potential hosts. Now work will begin to propagate these native fish species to return to the river system above the dam, which in turn should help the spectaclecase mussel reproduce and survive.

In Oregon and other parts of the West, while the western pearlshell is thought to be near threatened, the western ridged mussel seems to face the most threat. Overall, the population for this species seems to be on the decline, with its historic numbers and range depleted. Even with a limited historical record, sites where the western ridged mussel

---

1 Chris Rogers, "Discovery May Help Save Species," *Winona Post*, August 7, 2017.

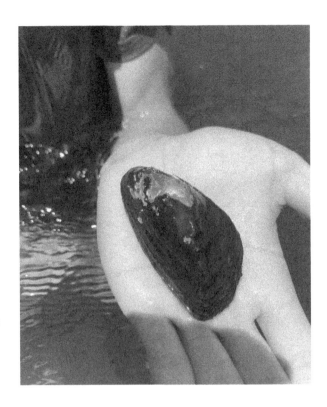

A very rare live western ridged mussel (*Gonidea angulata*); a bit smaller than western pearlshells, these have a distinctive ridge along the shell.

have been recorded have been revisited in recent years; in most cases the mussel presence has decreased, if not disappeared altogether. In Oregon additional research would be helpful to determine where, or whether, healthy populations exist outside of the known beds. In 2018, a study by my organization in the Eugene area on the Willamette found the first live western ridged mussel in that area of the Willamette mainstem. In 2020, another was found just on the edge of the Portland metro area, on a side channel of the mainstem Willamette. These were exciting finds, but in truth there has been far too little effort to search out where these mussels exist throughout multiple Oregon river systems.

In the Umatilla River in northeast Oregon, the western pearlshell was once thriving, and is considered a first food by the Confederated Tribes of the Umatilla Indian Reservation (CTUIR). It has been said that the Umatilla River was once full of pearlshells. In fact, archaeological evidence points to freshwater mussels being harvested in the area going back ten thousand years. Yet the modification of habitat and the significant use of water for irrigation, as well as other impacts, have caused those populations

A juvenile western pearlshell near Eugene.

to die off. Today the CTUIR is leading the way in artificially reproducing these mussels and reintroducing them to the river and surrounding areas that have been affected. The work is ongoing, with work being conducted at Walla Walla Community College's fisheries lab, where earlier similar work was conducted to reproduce vastly decreased lamprey populations.

I've sat along the Willamette and wondered at the myriad challenges that are presented to the western pearlshell mussel, the western ridged mussel, and the floater species (multiple species in the genus *Anodonta*). In those moments, my thoughts flicker over what seems like an endless expanse of potential detriments to their health. Obviously, their reproductive cycle is challenging enough in the best of conditions, but when we overlay the many influences that people have on our river systems, it is easy to see the increased difficulty we bring to freshwater mussels and many other species. All the changes that have been injected into the river environment—from the cleanliness of the water and modification of habitat to human-made chemicals applied across the landscape—mussels are on the receiving end of it all. Native freshwater mussels are at risk from our actions in a very direct fashion, seemingly every day.

Our societal romance with chemicals is something to ponder in relation to this animal. If you take a moment and simply look up the common term "pest control," you will quickly realize that such substances have become part of the economy. Pesticides are big business. They are used in many homes, gardens, and forests, and on large tracts of agricultural land; the chemical universe we have created pervades air, land, and water to an alarming degree. Pesticides have been developed and used in the name of killing insects, weeds, rodents, and myriad types of conditions that can affect crops. It is a very basic notion that when artificial substances are applied to the landscape, urban or rural, they can end up in the river by the simple action of rain—and of course the Willamette Valley receives a lot of rain. Water running across the landscape is pretty good at carrying pollutants, whether as free molecules in the water itself or bound to other particles. Pollutants, carried by runoff water, enter our creeks and our rivers and gain a direct connection to the myriad aquatic species found there. The Willamette, like a great many rivers, receives a huge amount of runoff.

Large quantities of pesticides are applied to the agricultural land that surrounds much of the Willamette River. If you add to that quantity similar chemical agents used in our cities, along our roadways, and in many other places, a logical conclusion is that mussels end up filtering some of that human-created mess that ends up in the river. Imagine being in one general area for decades, as mussels are, taking in polluted water, filtering it, and sending the filtered water back to the river. Imagine if that water being filtered by mussels carries a wide range of pesticides and herbicides in widely varying concentrations. Then combine these with other pollutants that enter the river. It does not take an aquatic biologist to wonder at what impacts such chemicals may have on the natural world.

Studies of a wide range of pesticides have shown very real effects on wildlife, from amphibians to mammals. Chemicals we inject into the natural world can have profound consequences on native species, from inhibiting their growth to limiting their reproduction. The average person may not think that the use of such agents causes harm to the natural world, or to themselves, but the degree to which our society has created markets for such products is simply profuse, and the effects are demonstrated in human and natural environments.

Too often, though, there is a lack of understanding of what the potential effects can be, and products are introduced into the market before all aspects of their potential effects are adequately analyzed. Additionally,

An adult western pearlshell on the right, with a tiny juvenile nestled into the river bottom just to the left of the adult.

many are reluctant to accept that we overuse such substances and have a lack of understanding about which products pose the greatest risk, not only to species in our rivers and creeks, like freshwater mussels, but also of course to human health. In Oregon, as in many other places, the state does relatively little to look into such issues, and the level of information about who sprays which products, and where they are used, is tightly controlled or, more commonly, unknown.

A few years ago, the US Geological Survey (USGS), an agency that should be held in high regard—yes, the same folks who care a lot about earthquake detection, natural hazards, and water levels—conducted a study of water quality in a first flush event. A "first flush" is in essence the first burst of rain after a dry period of weeks or months—typically giving a quick rise to creeks and rivers. In this case the USGS sampled water and sediment from a few creeks in Clackamas County to see what, if anything, could be found. In a blend of the dramatic and the expected, the suburban creeks yielded all kinds of toxic pollutants—many from home and yard use. One chemical in particular, bifenthrin, was found at high levels.

Bifenthrin is a chemical agent created to kill insects. Walk into a home or garden store in the spring and you will find products to "defend" your home, many of which contain bifenthrin. In fact, large displays are created at this time of year to drive sales of these kinds of products—as people contend with the "risks" associated with ants in their garage or a wily green plant growing at the edge of their driveway. Drama, coupled with the general fear that some people have of insects, is employed to sell this kind of product. It is ironic to think of someone "defending" their home against an often harmless insect, as the product they spray may well be degrading the survival of native species in the creek right outside their back doorstep.

In reality, that kind of mindset creates problems, some obvious and some less so. Bifenthrin happens to not be lethal to native fish, but guess what? It is quite lethal to native amphibians. It can kill the ants at your house and, potentially, the native salamander in your local creek. According to the USGS study, the creeks with the highest levels of bifenthrin contained the least amount of native amphibians. Research by USGS showed the link between use of such chemicals in our homes and their presence in the environment. Logical questions soon erupt, such as what else can such chemicals have an effect on? Does this stuff last once it is introduced into a creek? In fact, multiple potentially harmful pollutants were found in the USGS study, in addition to bifenthrin. It seems this study alone should be enough evidence that we collectively need to change our ways. Many other studies nationwide clearly indicate harmful effects by a range of other compounds.

When I think of the example of bifenthrin, I'm perplexed that this kind of product gets into the distribution chain at all. It makes little sense to sell anything that has the potential to kill native amphibians as a "side effect," just so an individual's version of an annoyance can be extirpated from the planet. The magnitude of this issue is not understood by enough people. How many other chemical products have a negative effect on the natural world and, of course, on the people that come into contact with it? In my experience, far too many products are used with little thought to the unacceptable risks they pose to you and me and the little creatures in our creeks and rivers.

In the realm of mussel research, a common herbicide called glyphosate (more commonly known as Roundup) was found in a 2007 study to cause impacts to juvenile mussels. Further, its other ingredients affect mature mussels.[2] Of course, many people believe glyphosate has multiple negative effects on human and environmental health—yet, again, it remains in wide use.

Many of the chemicals that find their way to our rivers every day are legally used but poorly understood. With everything that is known about the presence of a wide range of substances, it seems that more effort should be put into gaining information about what is present in water and sediment, which would then inform further action to curb pollution. Unfortunately, too often the opposite is true—the ability to look again, or to plan new sampling and testing, is too frequently hampered by lack of funds.

Who would think that in Oregon, this commonly described "green" state, the DEQ can screen and sample for toxics in the Willamette on average only every seven to eight years? Such decisions are controlled by the priorities of the agency itself, as well as the major imprint of the Oregon legislature. The level of lobbying against such testing has been historically intense from some industrial and agricultural interests. It seems these entities fear what can be found and revealed, and as a consequence, they seek to reduce the capacity of the DEQ and other agencies to deal with such issues.

This approach to the world—an approach that can affect the health of all species, including humans—is foolhardy. It is certainly not reflective of our historic "green ways." In recent times in the Oregon legislature, hardly a murmur is heard from any politician advocating for increased screening of our state's river for toxic substances. One thing to remember is that the timid response of our politicians, from governors on down to county commissioners, is dictated by the status quo—where even basic ideas that do not cost much to implement are shot down with ease. This is a key element of Oregon's green ways. Industries such as those surrounding pesticides have traditionally had more lobbyists and money behind them. It is a sad state of affairs in many ways, and one that people who made solid decisions in decades past would likely not tolerate.

The State of Oregon's often tepid approach to controlling and understanding pollution, and its unwillingness to robustly fund more research,

2   R. B. Bringolf, "Acute and Chronic Toxicity of Glyphosate Compounds to Glochidia and Juveniles of *Lampsilis siliquoidea* (Unionidae)," 2007, doi:10.1897/06-519R1.1.

made me think of a story I read a while back about mussels and efforts to recover them in Missouri. The article described the growing understanding that a wide range of pesticides can have a real negative impact on mussel species. Chris Barnhart, a malacologist and professor of biology at Missouri State University, seems to have said it best in relation to known effects from pollution and the need to better understand what chemicals can do to native species: "It's embarrassing how little we know about what's poison in the world," said Barnhart, in relation to the long list of chemicals that are present in our waters, with their influence on the natural world poorly understood.[3]

Mr. Barnhart's statement hits the nail on the head and reflects what many have said over the decades about the poisons we create and spread into the world, knowingly or otherwise. While much is known about certain legacy pollutants, such as DDT and PCBs, even these can be poorly characterized in river systems such as the Willamette, especially in relation to where they are still present, outside of a few well-known polluted areas. More troubling is the fact that newer realms of pollutants have seen relatively scarce study in river systems such as the Willamette. Pollutants such as flame retardants are showing up more regularly, some of which have a very similar chemical structure to PCBs.

When samples of sediment, water, and animal tissues are collected and screened, the relatively long list of findings, even at very low levels, are not analyzed for their impact to riverine species as a group. What interaction do such substances have collectively on fish, amphibians, and mussels? Looking at the list of pollutants identified in just the water itself from the upper Willamette River, one can wonder: What is the impact of the mixture of trichloroethane, estradiol, DDE, aldrin, atrazine, heptachlor, many kinds of PBDEs, and myriad other human-made chemicals? These are just a few of the dozens of chemicals identified in the water at Harrisburg on the upper river by the DEQ in 2007–2008. Results from a 2016 sampling conducted by the Oregon DEQ, the first since 2007–2008, were published in the fall of 2020; the work took four years to complete, thanks to not enough staff and equipment at the DEQ lab. The study revealed the usual suite of artificial substances in water, silt, and fish. Sure, these chemicals are found at parts per million and billion, but they

3 Stephen Ornes and Kathryn Whitney, "Resurrecting the Riverkeepers," bioGraphic, July 11, 2017.

are present all the same. The lack of analysis of the cumulative effects of all of these pollutants mixed together is problematic.

If we want to boil down what cumulative impacts are, it is easy. If the example is a human being, one can ask, what is the effect of inhaling diesel exhaust for a few hours a day, then eating fish with PCBs, then drinking water with glyphosate, and then eating food that contains high levels of growth hormones? Take all of them together and decide how they collectively affect health—that is an example of cumulative impact. There are many other combinations to play with in this hypothetical example. Looking at fish, or freshwater mussels, what is the result of many pollutants found in the water at the same time? If a mussel has to filter water containing minute amounts of bifenthrin, atrazine, glyphosate, DDE, heptachlor, and many other chemicals, what effect does this mixture have on a mussel? Heck, one can only wonder at the myriad additional chemicals found in the water far downstream, as more and more area for runoff is added. It makes swimming in the lower river seem a bit unappetizing.

With as much as we *do* know about which pollutants exist and how little characterization of them is typically done annually, even more embarrassing is the lack of desire by political leadership to do more to better understand what is poison in our world. That political reality is poison enough, I suppose. Oregon's green ways, in this vein, lack backbone.

Back in the river, somewhere on the upper Willamette along the side channel, that little mussel has been growing and maturing for years, filtering the river water nearly every minute of its life—and in all of that time it has been alive and growing. Under shallow rippling current in the summer months, with sunlight dappling through the shallows, it has held fast to the sand with its foot, nestling in among many larger shells. Here and there small native fish zip about, feeding at the river's edge. Native snails cling to the rocks against the persistent push of the current. All these little creatures have an unimaginably low level of say in these matters. Frankly, it is up to you and me to decide, and to work for change, on their behalf.

After seeing my first mussels on that channel back in 2001, it took only sixteen years to develop and implement a study of what appeared to be an unusual assemblage of mussels. The interest was always there, but it most certainly intensified when my organization gained management of the island in 2012. In the summer of 2017, a study was designed and conducted along the Norwood side channel to better understand the overall population of mussels in that local area. The study was designed by Celeste Searles Mazzacano, the PhD entomologist with an infectious enthusiasm for freshwater mussels. A collection of professionals and volunteers spent several days creating transects along the side channel, each person slogging and swimming up and down the channel to get the work done. From random starting points at the bottom of the channel, three series of transects were placed. Imagine a point on one side of the channel marked by flagging tape, and then an imaginary line extending from that tape across the channel. That is a transect. Generally, each series of transects was spaced every ten meters along the channel.

Each transect contained three randomly placed counts, from a weighted square called a quadrat. The distance from the shoreline for the placement of each quadrat was random, chosen ahead of time to enable a statistically random sample. When the quadrat was placed on the river bottom, the visible mussels were counted. About every third quadrat included the removal of the mussels from the top of the river bottom, then counting and measuring every one. Measuring the shell length can provide a basic age estimate for each mussel. After the removal of those on the surface, the sediment and rock were excavated a few inches into the river bottom to identify any juvenile or adult mussels that were below the surface. If found, these were measured and counted as well.

At times this kind of work can be taxing. Donning wetsuits and snorkels, the surveyors—with heads plunged into the cold current—carefully counted and removed the mussels. Then they dug into the substrate, slowly and methodically removing rocks and pebbles, seeking out additional mussels—especially juveniles, which can be found in the sediment. After the large items were cleaned from within the quadrat, each person carefully sifted through the sediment, sand, and rock, seeking any smaller shells. Their fingers moved slowly among the cloudy sand and silt, searching blindly at times for the oval shells. In the right conditions, most juvenile western pearlshell mussels remain in the river sediment for a few years as they grow from the tiny juveniles into large enough creatures to hold their own in the river current.

The crew worked this channel for three days, and each day brought some new wonders. In fact, at this place not only did the group find some amazingly old western pearlshell mussels that most likely can trace their nascent years back to the 1950s, but another species was found as well—the Oregon floater, which was a surprise to find in the quick-flow-ing water of the side channel. In the genus *Anodonta*, floaters are more commonly found in slower-moving waters, rich with deep sediment. Only a few occurred here, but their appearance seemed to prove the notion that where mussels can be found it not always easy to predict.

The findings from this study are interesting. Myriad large, old western pearlshell mussels dominated the counts and measurements. Unfortu-nately, no juvenile mussels were found in the collection of mussel beds along the one-mile side channel. Thousands upon thousands of large old pearlshells were identified, but a meaningful juvenile population was absent.

Many of the shells were deeply eroded, scarred, and worn away by decades of river flow. Abrasion by small rocks and larger ones likely con-tributed to the deep wear on the shells. The conclusion of this study is that there are up to forty thousand adult mussels on this side channel, yet there is no meaningful reproduction happening. From this study, many questions arose regarding why no juveniles were present.

Perhaps the host fish that helped build the massive bed was no lon-ger around, or perhaps the timing had changed when it was present, no longer coinciding with the release of the glochidia? Many similar ques-tions followed—all wondering at how such a large bed of mussels had no juveniles. Although it is certainly possible that host fish were carrying the glochidia elsewhere, it was very unusual to find a big bed with no juveniles.

Perhaps for some reason the massive bed on this side channel was not producing juveniles because of alterations of stream flow, or perhaps they were affected by changes in temperature? Given the multiplicity of new questions, further inquiry would be needed. It could also be that the mussels, which could well be at least seventy years old in some cases, were juvenile mussels around the time that the main US Army Corps dams were constructed on the Willamette's tributaries. What is known is that little analysis of freshwater mussels has occurred in relation to chemical pollutants. Over the next few years, it is likely that inquiry into the pres-ence of toxic chemicals in western pearlshells will be done.

In 2018 a similar crew of professionals and volunteers from my organi-zation conducted an analysis of an assemblage of mussel beds in Eugene. These beds are centrally located to downtown, adjacent to two islands.

A beautiful assemblage of western pearlshells on Thomas Creek, a sweet tributary to the Willamette that flows into the South Santiam River.

Over the course of three days, hundreds of mussels were counted and measured, similar to the approach taken in 2017 at Norwood, but along a shorter stretch of mainstem river of about four hundred meters. Unlike the results of the previous year, multiple smaller mussels were found! While they were not officially juvenile mussels of three centimeters or less, there were quite a few that were just above three centimeters and in the four-centimeter range.

Based on the findings, although the population is not characterized as robustly reproducing, it is officially viable. This was good news. Further inquiry will take place over the next few years, and perhaps beyond, to better understand these potentially long-lived creatures and how the many impacts to the Willamette River affect the few mussel species found there.

Although we have only a few mussel species compared with other parts of the United States, which have dozens, local and regional organizations seem to be taking increased note of these widespread mollusks. Associations of biologists and related professionals actively communicate with each other to strategize about new research, proposed research projects, and policy work that can have an impact on the health of freshwater mussels. In the Northwest, a consortium of folks has been meeting together for years to share information, circulate recently completed studies, and strategize about new work. Our understanding of mussels and other river species points to the need for better and more timely analysis, especially in relation to pollutants that enter the river.

6
Norwood Island Outpost

The one process now going on that will take millions of years to correct
is the loss of genetic and species diversity by the destruction of natural
habitats. This is the folly our descendants are least likely to forgive us.
— Edward O. Wilson, *Biophilia*

The old maps of the Irish Bend area make it clear why it is so named—you
can see the land ownership names of R. Yarborough, Nancy McGregor,
and so on, written in the distinct cursive of the time. Family names of
Irish origin are clearly printed on maps dating from 1853 and after. On
some the first surveys of the Willamette, Irish names appear on both sides
of the river in both Benton and Linn Counties, but there is certainly a
concentration around the area today known as Irish Bend. Viewing land
ownership along that stretch of river today, the original Irish names seem
to be mostly a thing of the past, yet many of the riverside lands that were
being worked back at that time are the same ones being cultivated in one
form or another today.

In 1853, the US General Land Office scoured the Willamette to get
a sense of the place and of course to seek to accurately depict what was
there. The drawings, jottings, and figures on their maps show a tangle
of riverlands, weaving and intermixing with channels moving south to
north, then winding west, then back again to the main current. Amid this
tangle, here and there the maps depict people trying to make a living off
the land.

Notations on the maps include entries such as "clay loam," with
myriad drawings of lowlands filled with water and riverside forests and
floodplain lands. Here and there, simple depictions of trees can be found
for the floodplain forest; in other areas, organized rows delineate early
orchards. In most cases the maps are pretty clear as to what the general
features of the river were at that time, either in text or in drawn figures

and symbols on the maps. Streams and backwaters show up regularly, and where the land along the river was being worked by some settler to produce potatoes, a rough square or rectangle has been drawn. The maps are available online and are a wonder to explore. I've spent probably far too much time examining these old documents, seeking to compare them to aerial photographs taken in recent years—a wondrous wormhole to travel down if you are not careful. At the same time, the ever-changing essence of the river is clear to see, as well as what changes have been brought by people.

In some cases, the course of the river has changed completely. Where you might see a small rivulet or side channel depicted on the General Land Office maps, today the entire river flows through what was once a creek-sized flow of water, with the old main channel as seen at that time now only a part of the floodplain on the other side of the river. I've sat sipping coffee in the morning at different Willamette campsites over the years, looking across the flow to the forest of willow, ash, and cottonwood, knowing in some cases that the old main channel used to flow more than three hundred meters out of my view, or perhaps farther out. Today big cottonwood trunks hold fast to the rocky soil where the river once flowed. In those moments, if I was to transport myself back in time, I wouldn't be sitting at the water's edge with my feet pressing against rounded river rock—instead I'd be sitting on the soil of the forest, perhaps with my back against a cottonwood, hearing the main river flowing somewhere out yonder beyond my view.

At the place that today we call Norwood Island is a big bend in the river, facing west. By 1861, when another cartographic effort was put forth, the maps show a slight channel cutting through the neck of land on the inside bend to the east. An "inside bend" is basically this: if you are traveling down the river, and there is a curve in the river—say the channel moves from south to north, winding to the west and then back to the east—that land on the right, the inside of the bend, is the inside of the river bend. Characteristically, the water along the bend runs more slowly, or often has an eddy.

In this case, that old inside bend would soon be a larger version of today's Norwood Island, as that small channel became the main channel cutting through the neck of land—or oxbow. That is when the island was created. Whether that occurred because of a high flow or a flood, or was

A bit of island isolation for this blacktail buck at Norwood, early May.

instead just enlarged slowly over time, we will never know for sure. It may have been a big flood in the 1800s, or one of more common dimensions, but that knowledge is beyond the existing maps and written accounts. When that small channel became the main channel, it still left a vibrant side channel all the way to the west, thus creating one good-sized island of a few hundred acres at least. The 1861 map provides a good sense of it.

General Land Office and Corps of Engineers surveys back in the 1800s that generated the first maps of the river, and many others, are efforts worthy of significant respect. Imagine members of the General Land Office survey, carrying a variety of gear into unknown waters, with none of the modern methods of route finding, with no way to communicate long distances from the river. It was a pretty amazing effort, put forward in a time when muscle and determination were the greatest assets.

As Norwood first became an island, the main channel was still situated to the west. As the small channel to the east grew, over time it became the main channel. This configuration seems to have lasted for about eighty years. Between 1955 and 1964, the main channel made a big shove to the west in what appears to be one or two significant reroutings. It is conceivable this was due to flooding, and likely the flood of 1964 played a role in what the island is today. Since that time, the area has been pretty much in its current alignment, with an island of about eighty acres, and the adjoining property to the east that borders where the main channel once flowed.

The island and surrounding land is indeed floodplain. It is relatively low and receives floodwater that can backflow onto the island from the Long Tom River confluence along the side channel, or from the main river when things get higher. In 2015, about 70 percent of the island was covered briefly with a flow of about 65,000 cubic feet per second as measured by the Harrisburg, Oregon, river gauge. Aerial photos taken by a friend of the 2015 event show a brown swath of water expanding over the downstream end of the island, with a few isolated areas still standing above the flow—the little islands on an island. In 2016, 2017, and 2018, the island remained a few feet above the highest flows. Norwood East, the area across today's main channel on the inside bend, receives regular injections of winter flows that permeate the riverscape—with all manner of small backwaters coming to life at different points of the winter and spring. In 2019, likely 95 percent of the island was covered by the strange mid-April flood that saw the Harrisburg gauge rise to 70,000 cfs. It was a very odd event, with masses of brown floodwater swirling against many riverside trees that were flowering. At the time I could only think of the many examples of wildlife displaced or killed by that event, in addition of course to the hardship experienced by the surrounding landowners.

Ecologically, the area around Norwood is rich. The slow-moving and meandering Long Tom flows into today's side channel from the west. Often this small Willamette tributary pours in very turbid water, based on the operations of the Fern Ridge Dam, a few miles upstream. The side channel around the island is lush with native riparian vegetation on the island side, which is atypical in relation to much of the river. Summer months find much of the main channel just a couple feet deep in some areas, with fast-moving clear water. On the mainstem side, the channel is wide and relatively shallow. Here I've seen chinook migrating upstream on late spring days, swimming along the shoreline, a few here and a couple there, far from historic numbers. The movement and ecological elements of the river here are compelling, but Norwood has an additional storyline of merit.

For decades a family grew crops on the island, up until the late 1990s. From what the previous landowners describe, it was a mix of crops, from corn in some years to grass seed in others. All of this was made possible by a bridge that connected across the side channel just upstream of the Long Tom River confluence, built sometime in the 1950s. Here tractors could make their way across to the large flat island expanse. Reviewing aerial photos, it appears that, during the prime farming period on the island, it was nearly all cultivated—flat and devoid of native trees and shrubs.

I learned of Norwood Island and its ownership back in 2002 from a friend who said the landowner might let us use it for a big paddle event we conducted. The owners had stopped farming it after the 1996 flood damaged the bridge, though it was potentially useable for vehicles smaller than large tractors. We visited the island more than once to see if it would work for our needs. At one point we took a small tractor and truck across the rickety old wood bridge along the side channel to clear some invasive weeds for access and to see if the island could host a large group. After a few hours of work, our trip back across the bridge proved treacherous. Initially we walked back across the bridge, testing the timbers and some

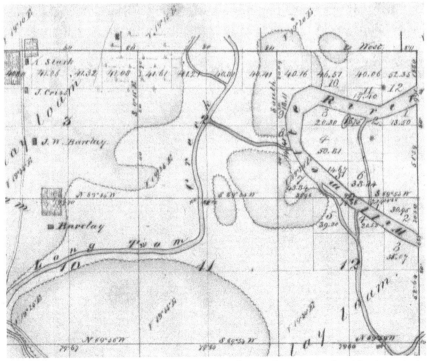

The old General Land Office Survey Map shows the very beginning of an island at today's Norwood Island area.

of the wood we had used to resurface portions of the bridge that morning. After a few steps, a large timber fell from beneath the bridge's surface. With such a loud splash of wood hitting the water, I was surprised we didn't get wet. The structure was a true mess—a reality we had glossed over as we crossed it initially. The flood of 1996 had done its job, as had high water events in subsequent years. It had been an unwise choice to cross the bridge that day, and now we had to head back.

Trepidation gripped us as my friend got ready to drive the borrowed tractor back across, and me in a large Ford F-350 dually. As my friend crossed, pieces of the bridge fell away. At one point the tractor tire poked through the surface; we carefully guided the machine back out of the hole, and around it. I raced back to the truck after he had crossed. The diesel rumbled, and I hit the pedal. If this thing was to land in the channel, I wanted it to be as close to the shoreline as possible to be retrieved. With the pedal slammed down, the engine roared to life, and the big truck whisked across the groaning timbers. Thankfully, we made it across. That was it— the island would henceforth be a true island, inaccessible by land except for a few daring folks willing to walk over the decaying bridge. Looking back on those lucky moments in life, sometimes you just have to smile. In

Another sweet spot to pitch a tent along the river.

the mid-2000s, high water brought massive amounts of large wood down the channel. Large trees and root wads did their work, and after a time, the bridge was completely gone. Today only a few pilings remain.

Farming was at an end on Norwood. Shortly after our foolish escapade to the island, in the early 2000s, the landowners entered into an agreement to plant and grow native plants on the island—those that grow naturally in Oregon. The federal government would pay them a yearly sum to plant and grow thousands of native trees and shrubs, instead of raising crops, in an effort to establish natural habitat, or at least habitat that was a marked improvement over grass seed and other crops that had much less value to native birds, fish, and mammals. In such programs, the goal is to improve conditions for fish and wildlife over time, gradually restoring the land to a more natural state. Many thousands of plants were put in the ground with the aid of a conservation partner over a single planting season. It was an impressive effort that resulted in a range of native species that survive on the island today.

Establishing an intertwined and connected mosaic of green along the river's floodplain was the goal at Norwood, and that is the basic goal of many similar projects being conducted along the river today. Native riverine species like Oregon ash, the Willamette Valley variant of the ponderosa pine, various species of willow, and many native shrubs that thrive along the floodplain were planted at Norwood, species from Douglas spirea and Nootka rose to serviceberry and ninebark. In this case the job was, and is, even more difficult to complete given the former use of the island. Decades of agricultural production means that the soil has been greatly modified from what it once was, and the seedbank in the soil of Norwood today is replete with invasive plants—a wide mix of species seeking to grow among the native species planted more than eighteen years ago.

In 2007 or so, my organization looked at ways to improve habitat on Norwood Island, beyond what the landowner had already done. Together, the work of planting tens of thousands of plants on the island and some additional effort would yield good results for native biodiversity there. Norwood and the area around it was known to fish biologists at that time to have some very good habitat, and the potential for more plants that were historically common along the river, along with structures such as large wood—large woody debris, now more frequently called coarse woody detritus (CWD)—would benefit salmon, cutthroat trout, and all kinds of other wildlife that had been common along the Willamette's rich floodplain for millennia. CWD is in essence fallen trees, root wads, and other wood material found in naturally functioning river systems, but too often less frequently found in highly managed river systems. With the small river flowing into the side channel that formed the island, the offerings of the island itself, the main channel just a long rock-throw to the east, and the natural floodplain on the river's east side, the complex was very interesting.

Finding funding for additional work in the early 2000s was problematic, but we kept in touch with the landowner for several years. Even so, it came as a bit of a surprise to get a phone call from him in 2013. I retuned his call, and he told me he wanted to offer the island to my organization. Over time, the combination of advocacy, education, and scientific work for the river had gained us some good landowner friends. We agreed on a price that we both thought was fair and entered into a deal that would provide us with full ownership of the island by the end of 2017. It was the right thing for the river and would continue to enhance the ability for wildlife to thrive there and for people to gain an improved connection with the beauty of the river. It also included a key element of the public trust, in a nonprofit owning the property, in keeping with the original Greenway concept.

In 1971, when the Willamette Greenway program was just trying to bloom from a new idea into something that provided public property along the river, it was moving slowly. The glacial growth of the program inspired a proposal for five focal parks along the Willamette, instigated (as described by Bauer) by Glenn Jackson, the powerful chair of the Oregon Transportation Commission. At the same time, the state was ready to make a big move to establish several Greenway parks along the Willamette River, after the grant program for local municipalities did not reach the envisioned goal in terms of the volume of land acquisition.

The proposals included creating a park in Eugene called Dexter Dam, today called Elijah Bristow; one near Albany called Lower Kiger, today called Bowers Rock; Lone Tree Bar was next, today known as Willamette Mission just north of Salem; and Molalla-Pudding River was next, today's Molalla River State Park, just outside the City of Canby. The fifth proposed was Norwood Island State Park—yes, Norwood Island was proposed as one of the five major state parks in 1971!

The northern half of Norwood Island and its long arc.

While the island is about eighty-five acres today, the proposed park was more than a thousand acres, meaning that it would have spanned hundreds of additional acres on both sides of the river. When I first learned of this, I was pretty astonished; Webb Bauer's thesis was the first I'd read of this. Even more astonishing is that I hadn't known this until after we developed the agreement with the landowners to purchase the island; they had purchased the property in 1979 and had not heard of the state park proposal either. Learning of this decades-old proposal for Norwood felt like finding a missing link in the Willamette Greenway story. You see, Norwood Island was adjacent to property owned by the Van Leuwen family, who turned out to be one of the major opponents of additional public land along the Willamette. Some of the Van Leuwen family's property was included in the proposal—which naturally did not sit well with them. This history was well documented in a story by *Oregon Field Guide* on OPB in 2012.

Liz Van Leuwen became the organizer and main political opponent of the Greenway in the early 1970s. Her efforts were significant, result-ing in a collection of like-minded others who were against the State of

Oregon purchasing more land for the public along the Willamette. Her efforts helped decrease the breadth of potential public lands along the river. Perhaps more importantly, their efforts helped to recast the intentions of the State of Oregon at that time.

Elements of strong opposition were in place before 1971, but it certainly seems that the proposal for Norwood Island State Park raised the collective fear to a new level, with uncertainty about the State of Oregon taking land via eminent domain. Additional visions of a bunch of hairy "hippies" floating down the river and trespassing on people's land elevated discontent with the proposal. As with many things then, and more broadly in our current time, fear seems to capture the people's imagination. Missing a few critical facts, the notion of what may or may not happen in a particular instance can gain a life of its own, especially when certain concepts are repeated over and over, whether they are fact or fiction.

Unlike many human relations today among those who may disagree about particular issues, my interactions with Mrs. Van Leuwen were always cordial. My time working on the Willamette occurred later in her life, and when I'd meet her at a public meeting or a talk, she was always polite—even if she disagreed with what I was saying. She might give me a bit of a ribbing about something I had said in public, but she always seemed to have a bit of a grin when she did so. Frankly, she has a likable personality. It was easy for me to see why she had become a successful politician while serving as a representative in the Oregon legislature for many years. In some ways her attitude, or at least her ability to act in a civil fashion, corresponds with how Governor Straub and Governor McCall had publicly and collegially responded toward a proposal that had originally been put forward by only one of them.

Straub was a Democrat and McCall a Republican, yet that was not an issue—their every response was not necessarily dictated by ideology or tied to the accepted carefully vetted talking point of the day. In the case of the Greenway proposal, they both agreed to support it, whichever one prevailed in the coming election. Not to get too nostalgic about noteworthy people and politics of the past, but perhaps you will indulge this bit of sentimental imagining: we are not so very far from that time. It may well be more than fifty years since the original Greenway proposal, yet even though people certainly had strong feelings about things in those decades, as they do now about a range of topics, it didn't always spill over into our regular public discourse as it seems to do today as a matter of practice. If we think about the efforts since that time to provide enough funding to sample the river for toxic contaminants, or to purchase public land, those efforts have been consistently stung by the instant reaction of a political faction—rather than approached as efforts that can be generally supported because the ideas behind them have real value.

It just may be that, in another era, civility was more prominent. Basic discussion did not devolve immediately into a political position, with one "side" clearly being the spawn of the devil. It may also reflect a time when people understood the definition of and importance of facts—things that are true, verifiable, indisputable, and so on. It may also reflect a time when people checked facts themselves—verifying what was true, or not, which can go a long way toward keeping nonsense out of the public discourse. It also seems that the consideration of what is good for all, versus what is good for only a few, was more prominent in the minds of people generally, and politicians of any perspective as well. As Mr. Vonnegut might have said, shaking his head, "and so it goes."

As I look back on this past era for the Willamette, and on all the years since, it may be that the proposal for Norwood Island State Park was a distraction, an easy place to focus the anger of Greenway opponents as other proposals for public lands along the river came into being. Ultimately, the pushback by folks in Linn County, according to Webb Bauer and

The beautiful assemblage of pines along the eastern edge of Norwood Island. These are the Willamette Valley variant of the ponderosa pine.

Nellie fully immersed
in the daisies of June on
Norwood.

others, was intense enough to have the proposal for Norwood as a state
park dropped from the mix.

These days some of the ponderosa pines planted in the early 2000s
are more than twenty feet tall and provide ample amounts of sweet shade
on hot summer afternoons—contrary to my initial reaction in 2004, when
it seemed that those trees, so low in the floodplain, might not have done
too well. You can look out at the river, see an osprey diving for a fish in
the shallow summer water, or hear the great birds calling to each other as
they circle overhead. With chirping calls the osprey seem to converse and
hunt with vigor, with one a hundred feet above the river, and its partner
circling fifty feet higher, watching the progress of the bird scanning for a
silhouette of a fish below.

During late summer, when the flows of the river are lowest, the depth
of the main channel here is only a couple of feet. If you know where to
go—and let me tell you there is no guarantee to this statement—you can
get across the river by foot. One time I did this at the very lowest summer
flows, hefting a long beaver-chewed staff to stabilize me. Now, don't get

me wrong, wading across the mainstem Willamette is usually not a great idea. Having paddled all over the area in my canoe over the years, I had developed a somewhat sound notion of where to step, and where not to, and generally what to expect. There was one line along the whole channel that might work.

Wearing my lifejacket, also known as a personal floatation device or PFD, was part of my drill even in the heat of summer paddling a canoe. Varying undulations in the river bottom, some rocks slick with algae, and the sheer force of the current, even in the low levels of high summer, would make the effort tricky, even holding the beaver-fashioned staff. Water as a force of nature is a strange and wonderful thing, but it is something to always be cognizant and respectful of. It is also important to note that, given the size of the array of round stones, with no bedrock to speak of, foot entrapment risk was minimal. One must always be cognizant of getting a foot stuck in some hole in the river rock. Here the rounded and occasionally moving stones presented minimal risk on my chosen route.

I started on the upper end of the island, stepping carefully over the rocks, placing my sandaled feet gently on the river bottom. One step at a time, staff moving up and down to gain a hold in front of me, then left foot, then right foot, then another placement of the staff, searching out contours on the river bottom that might suddenly drop me another foot or two into the water. At one point the depth increased, and I nearly turned back. My feet rested on rocks the size of my foot, interspersed with many smaller ones that form the river bottom there, mixed with large granular sand and fine brown river silt. As I neared the willowy expanse of the east bank, the depth increased for a few meters, making every step a careful choice. At one point I was nearly knocked over. I moved with the current, stepping slowly downriver and across, and soon the depth decreased and I was there, standing among the outstretched leaves of the healthy willows.

I didn't stay long, and carefully repeated the exercise back the other way, aiming a bit more downriver this time toward the main part of the Norwood Island campsite. Left, right, then walking stick. Left right, then walking stick, with a quick splash into the flow to a crisp spack to the river bottom. After a bit I was thigh-deep in running water, then nearly waist-deep. One step, then another, and after a bit the flow was more shallow and the energy of the water less robust. A few more steps and I was on the shoreline, smiling a bit and looking back across the beautiful ever-moving current. It was a feat only the low water of early August could provide. Since that time, the channel has changed, and the east side is deeper, making such a trek pretty tough unless you plan to swim.

At any rate, I've been to the island a lot over the past few years. It is both a place to get work done for the river and, at the end of a long day, a place that's very peaceful. Often it is quite relaxing, well-suited to clearing the mind. In fact, I got married there in the summer of 2020 during the pandemic—which was simply perfect! Eloping there with my wife, daughters, and a couple of friends was ideal, in the face of plans getting derailed time and again by changing conditions. The many flowers on the island were in full bloom, from the Nootka rose and Douglas spirea providing bursts of color to the beautiful daisies at their peak. For us, Pine Camp was the perfect riverside perch from which to exchange our vows. We will remember the island, and the amazing riverine immersion, for all of our days.

7
Hidden Beauty

A house built on greed cannot long endure.
—Edward Abbey, *Postcards from Ed: Dispatches and Salvos from an American Iconoclast*

If rivers are left alone, free of dams, and if hard structures along the riverbank are few and far between, big meandering rivers can do what they have always done. By the very nature of rising and falling waters, rivers naturally move up and across the floodplain, extending their aquatic reach, refilling backwaters, and spreading nutrients. Up until about 150 years ago, the Willamette's general course kept the same complex weave of channels, with the river spreading east and west along the floodplain as a normal seasonal pattern.

The *floodplain*, typically defined as the area of lowlands adjacent to a river—sometimes small and constrained by hillsides, sometimes wide and open for miles—is really an integral part of any fully functioning and healthy river. In the case of the Willamette, historically the river was full of rich backwaters that could extend far inland on either side of the river, creating rich habitat woven of green willows, thick blockades of Nootka rose, and rising walls of Oregon ash. Side channels wove along roughly parallel to the mainstem or *stems* of the river. In some cases, two channels of roughly the same size would wrap around an island, surging back together two hundred meters downstream or, at times, several miles downstream.

When the river maintains its natural function, habitats that nourish fish, myriad bird species, and buckets of other wildlife along the river are interlinked to the surge of the spring flow and the arrival of longer and warmer days. One of the most significant changes began to occur along the river when people placed structures along the riverbank to constrain the river's natural spread into its side channels and floodplain. Materials used for this effort to trap the river were large rocks heaped against the riverside, known as riprap. Large wood pilings were also used along the bank, and at the opening of side channels, to keep more water in the main channel. From the earliest settlement of Euro-American visitors along the river in the 1800s, and for decades after, the struggle to tame the river was to some degree ongoing. This is a story common to many rivers across the United States. Over time, these containment efforts were stoked at the local, state, and federal levels, with work conducted by individuals, towns, state and federal governments, or all of the above. Work to control rivers like the Willamette often focused on engineered structures to defend against a river's natural tendency for wanderlust.

All the work to keep the river to one main channel, to limit its seeming natural desire to spread outward at higher flows, has had a direct connection to the health of wildlife species along the Willamette, from fish like spring chinook to birds like the yellow-billed cuckoo that no longer flourish along the Willamette because of habitat loss. Over the past few decades, the story has not changed all that much. Riprap is still used, but it is now intermingled with stream barbs—piles of large rock at the river's edge that are constructed to create an eddy behind them that, in the right alignment of flow and geomorphology, can protect the riverbank downstream. Sometimes they work, but often they do not.

Viewing old maps gives one a sense of the river's change. The advent of aerial photography, which began many decades ago, provides another perspective for understanding the landscape of the formerly tangled river. Much newer technology, such as Lidar, yields a more fine-grained view of what the river was, and what it is today. Typically radiating downward from specially equipped aircraft, Lidar sends pulse waves of laser light that penetrate fairly close to the ground. The many waves are analyzed to provide the elevation of the ground where the pulses make contact, resulting in a 3D image that reveals slight depressions, contours, channels, and textures. Although Lidar does not provide images that reflect differences in inches or millimeters, it does reveal, if the waves can get to close the ground, the difference in elevation in a fashion that provides detail that had previously been, if not unobtainable, exceedingly difficult to gain at any scale beyond in-person, up-close examination.

Looking at Lidar images of the river floodplain, you can see the present river channels in fine detail. Among these images, you might witness a long arc of an area, depressed a few feet in depth and depicted in a different

color, in a present-day farm field. These lines often represent the old channels, revealed by Lidar. The technology and the image produced enable
us to peer into the past and see the old weaving ways of the river, from how
the main channel moved west or east to old oxbows that used to connect
to the main river's flow. Many of the old channels revealed by Lidar are
today seemingly stranded hundreds of meters from the main river, with
water reaching them only at the highest flood. You can see them from an
airplane, but by pairing them with the many other channels revealed by
Lidar, the generations of being cut off from the river and overall discon-
nection makes more sense in many cases. At times the images provide a
glimpse of what could be again—with alternations to river management
and new restoration actions that could one day take place.

Restoration projects can open up some of these old channels, and
potential projects span the range, from the complex to the very basic
in design. One key principle is to open up old blocked channels that
might still gain water during normal high spring flows. In some cases, it
is a relatively simple matter of excavating out an old earthen plug put in
place decades back. Such action might enable a channel that presently
has water for three weeks of the spring flow to become a channel that
contains water for eight weeks—providing more habitat for a range of
fish, mammals, and birds. In some places the river seems very close to
reconnecting with some of these features on its own, perhaps being only
one modern flood away from pushing out across the floodplain and being
brought back to life.

Hoacum Island today is a highly affected area—a relatively low floodplain island that has been largely converted to agriculture over the past 150
years. Along much of this island, agricultural fields stretch to the river's
edge, leaving few native trees and shrubs separating the cultivated from
the rippling current. Yet even with significant change over the decades,
and modification of floodplain habitat, in this area you can still see small
but important glimpses of the old Willamette, with the small Greenway
property on the northwest corner of the island being the prime example.

Paddling our canoe just north of Sam Daws Landing in the summer
of 2015, we reach a small channel, nearly unnoticeable, that begins on
river left, the west side of the river. Across the river to the east the first
green fringes of the Snag Boat Bend Unit of the William Finley National
Wildlife Refuge begin. Snag Boat Bend is a nice complex of backwater

habitat that supports western pond turtle and other native species. Joining me on his day off was my friend Scott Youngblood, who was also the river ranger for Oregon Parks.

As we entered the small channel in Scott's canoe, the morning was blue sky with the sounds of birds and rippling current all around. For any paddler with a bit of knowledge, it is well known that small, relatively narrow channels like Hoacum can be dangerous when there is deep, fast current. During high flows, it is not uncommon for trees to fall, resulting in a blockage of all or part of the channel. Such an obstacle forces you to get out of your craft and haul yourself, along with boat and gear, around the obstruction—if you are lucky enough to have that option. Depending on the size and amount of other wood or root wads that may be present, it can be an adventure. If the main channel is high, the side channels will be high as well, with the risk from such debris increasing dramatically. By contrast, on this summer trip, the water was shallow, and the paddling was relatively carefree.

In a serpentine weave across the miles of low floodplain landscape, the small channel crosses through an expanse of tilled land. Here mint, grass seed, and other crops grow along the river. Occasionally I could glimpse the acreage through a gap in the vegetation, and sometimes the flat, tilled expanse seemed to go on forever to the west. On this day we noted some very healthy native vegetation in places along the island's bank, and in other sections an invasive wall of Himalayan blackberry and reed canary grass reached upward in an untamed mass. Sometimes these species seemed to rise into the native vegetation—highlighting their efficient outcompeting aptitude for shading out the small native wildflowers and shrubs and rising faster toward the sunlight.

Our goal this day was Hoacum Island Greenway, a property of about forty acres located on the northwest corner of the island. It is owned by the Oregon Parks and Recreation Department and is part of the Willamette River Greenway program. Isolated and small, this little outpost of green and brown amid a sea of agricultural fields holds fast against the incoming flow of tractor-tilled and herbicide-coated annual crops nearby. Like others, Hoacum Greenway is an island on an island.

We worked our way along the gurgling side channel, hopping out of the canoe on occasion to lift it over a small gravel bar, then jumping back at the right water depth. These quick interludes of getting out of the boat

Hoacum Island Landing, on the far northwest bend of the larger island.

and back in were also used to scan the river bottom above and below the gravel bars, looking for western pearlshell mussels, native fish, and, of course, agates. On the upper end we identified a few western pearlshells. It was an easy pattern: paddle for a bit, examine the plants and the open spots along the shoreline, as well as the fish and macroinvertebrates on the river bottom, then hop out when only a couple inches of water made it over the pebbles. Skim the canoe along the shallows, scan the channel for a bit, then get back in.

Like most rivers, rock has its place along the Willamette—from large formations here and there to the myriad rounded rocks that shape the channel bottom. River rocks of various sizes, shapes, and colors could be seen along this channel, some including big doses of volcanic red and others with hints of pale green. These dots of color were mixed among the dark gray and black rounded volcanic rocks that are the dominant ingredient. Here and there one could see petrified wood, and a range of other interesting rocks.

On this day, the simple pleasure of scanning for cool rocks was part of the "work." I had gained a true love of looking for unique rocks, but it was an activity that had not always been interesting to me. Over the years I had watched people collect rocks from quite a few rivers, an activity that had never really challenged my imagination. Frankly, in some ways it seemed like a waste of time. The strange thing is that I've always been fascinated by geology, with its vast timescales, its unique and myriad stories of particular geologic regions, and its epic story of the continents and the Earth's crust. To me the "descriptive science" has always been full of interesting observations, stories, and theories. From plate tectonics and volcanic events to fault block mountain ranges and vast erosional processes, it all challenged my sense of time, to say the least. In recent decades the science of geology has become more complex, as well, adding increased precision to geologic timescales and processes. But rocks along the river, so what? There are billions of them. Birds, fish, freshwater mussels, aquatic plants, algal blooms, and riverside forest, those were the things of interest. That's not to say that I don't appreciate stretching out on a newly shaped gravel bar with my camera to photograph the untouched state of a new, naturally artful rise in the gravel just revealed by decreasing flows. In the spring, when the waters recede, the newly revealed patterns of the rocks, with long sweeping depressions and slight upheaval, leave beautiful arrangements along the river. Agates though—it was hard to understand why anyone cared. So, although agate hunting didn't hook me in the beginning, it seems there have always been groups of people who love to search them out.

Barbara May, who has paddled rivers with groups of people for years along the Willamette, has long been a rock hound. Typically, when she leads canoeists and kayakers down the Willamette, they do not move fast, taking a rather pokey pace—if any pace at all. The determined slowness of her group trips is due largely to their frequent stops. Most any gravel bar of consequence acts like a magnet for Barbara and her group, and they simply cannot resist stopping to take a look. You see, there may well be agates to be found!

Nearly every gravel bar that has the slightest resemblance to one that has been shifted and molded by the river's current over the previous season draws them in. Thousands upon thousands of rocks being moved around by winter and spring high water can create a fresh field of exploration, with agates brought to the surface that have not seen the light of day in millennia, if ever. The natural canvas may be the same as last year, or it may well be vastly different, depending on the seasonal flows. In some cases, new gravel bars reveal themselves, to add to the opportunity. The key is, you only know whether this canvas is new or not by stopping and carefully looking.

Endless scouring of the river bottom is a predictable occurrence with unpredictable endpoints. River channel morphology is the study of the shape, boundary, and characteristics of a river channel, and how it changes over time. In the case of the Willamette and many other rivers, the story is one of change, which most certainly involves gravel bars. Now, if you can't visualize a gravel bar, picture, basically, a long stretch of river gravel that sometimes forms a shoreline of the river in various widths, and at other times forms a distinct island of gravel in the middle of the river, or to one side or the other. Of course, depending on the flow level of the river, such shapes are revealed by the low flows of summer and at other times are never seen, concealed by their depth. Because the mediums in question are water, rock, silt, sand, and, at times, wood, the resulting energy and movement are dynamic and more or less prone to ongoing change. Sometimes the shape-shifting aspect of the river provides a range of benefits for people.

At times a whole new gravel bar appears where one hasn't been seen ever, usually caused by high flows. The City of Harrisburg had never had a large gravel bar before about 2005. Their city boat ramp entered open water that stretched a long way downstream along the east bank of the river; accessing the river on this stretch was done primarily via this one entry point to open water—for power boats, canoes, drift boats, kayaks, and anything else. Harrisburg had no beach, and typically only a relatively steep bank down to the waterline that didn't enable access for the average person. After a long stretch of winter flows, in the span of one wet season, the formerly open water near the river's eastern edge received enough gravel to create a massive gravel bar from the boat ramp, at the upstream end, to a point some four hundred meters downstream, as seen during low summer flows. At the time, city leaders were shocked, as were some Harrisburg residents. Initially plans for a new boat ramp had to be scrapped, and there was some grumbling about the impact of this gravel bar on the city's plans. As winter transitioned into spring and summer and river levels dropped, it soon became evident to most everyone that the gravel bar was a community benefit: although the gravel bar made launching a trailered boat a bit more tricky without a four-wheel-drive vehicle, it provided a vast new area for river access that had been nowhere to be found within the city limits before. In one fell swoop, the river brought the people of Harrisburg closer to it, and the people have enjoyed it ever since. Each year, as soon as the water is low enough, people gravitate to the gravel bar and can be seen there throughout the warm-weather season. With high flows at some future time, the gravel bar could shift again—time will tell.

As new gravel bars form along the river, or when existing ones are altered significantly, a corresponding feeling of opportunity is awakened for agate hunters. Most often the rocks most prized along the river are the carnelian agates. These are the translucent rocks that have banding and often burst with color. Carnelians along the Willamette are typically reddish, white, or orange, and all have some level of translucence—glass-like is one way to think of them. These form when a cavity in a rock, typically lava in the case of our area, is slowly filled in with silica and mineral impurities. The collection of silica molecules can eventually form crystals. Over time, these layer together, filling the cavity, or at least

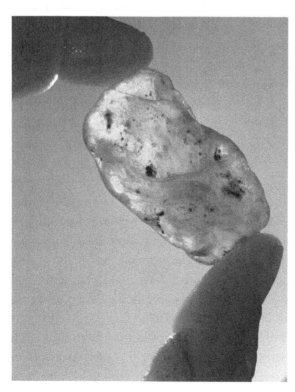

A vibrant red-orange translucent agate.

a portion of it. If the minerals have the right hue, their colors can radiate and sparkle. After the lava cools, and many years go by, such rocks can be broken apart, exposing the contents of the formerly empty pocket.

Over millennia, some of these rocks erode away from where they were formed and find their way far downhill, flushed by spring runoff. In some instances, agates might have been carried great distances on chunks of ice; the Bretz floods are a prime example of high waters reaching into the Willamette Valley thousands of years ago. However they are transported, eventually these brilliantly colored ornamental rocks can end up along the river. If you know where to look, these beauties can be found in a whole variety of places inland as well. Along the Willamette, I've occasionally found beautiful carnelian orange agates, which are blessed with a good dose of the mineral citrine. Others are deep red, but translucent and bright when held up to sunlight. Depending on where you are, many variations can be found glimmering along the surface of a gravel bar. At the end of the day, there are many beautiful rocks of all colors, shapes, and textures.

For Barbara's group, which frequently searches for interesting rocks along the river, the pattern goes something like this. After securing their canoes and kayaks along the rocky shoreline, the group embarks in a disorganized fashion along the gravel bar, fanning out in wayward patterns headed upstream and down. Some travel inland and some walk the shoreline, yet all have their heads down, scanning the dry rocks as well as the ones just under the water's surface. Patterns of searching can vary to the point of amusement. I've seen some people in her group (and others) zigzag as they walk, while others creep along an invisible straight line, scanning a patch of ground ten feet wide, then turn and repeat—as if they were operating a lawn mower, stacking row after row as they search. All the while, these people are keen to any sparkle or glint of color among the more muted gray rocks, or the bleached rocks of summer. If something looks promising, perhaps a bright rock covered with dried algae, they nudge it with their foot or reach down for a quick pickup. When one is found, it is typically held high toward the sun to gauge the degree of translucence. Each person seems to take pride in their approach—some demonstrating an intriguing combination of efficiency and creativity. Sometimes the agates are simply not present at a particular beach or gravel bar, and the group must toss back any small rocks they may have found and concede defeat. At other times a couple people in the group might walk along a stretch that has the feel of an agate "vein." Every few feet they may find something, while someone walking just ten feet to the right on a parallel line will find nothing. This is the way of agate hunting.

James T. is another one hooked by interesting rocks. Each and every trip on the river involves stopping to look at pretty much any gravel bar that has not been examined by him in a while. As a result, the guy has a rock collection that is top notch! Reaching beyond the natural beauty of these rocks, James is sure to take the less amazing agates that he finds and put them into a rock polisher, where additional beauty is revealed. He would admit the whole endeavor is a perfect kind of hobby. A pursuit that combines paddling a canoe along a gorgeous river, enjoying the natural world, and finding the little nuggets of natural wonder—what could be better?

It seems that the strong hook that sends people searching for agates and other interesting rocks is elemental. When some river jewel is found, a person naturally wonders about the others—assuming they are somewhere nearby. Where are they, and why do they occur here? Is this a vein of sorts that I can trace? Did some massive chunk of ice from a big flood make it to this point one hundred miles up the Willamette Valley and finally give away this radiant prize, or was it the push of flow from high in the Cascades? I resisted such nonsense questions for years, and at times shook my head at the time-consuming practice, never seeing the point. I mean, bird-watching, now that can tell you something about a place, and can be an indicator of the ecological function of a landscape to some degree—that seems worthy of time and energy. But looking for shiny translucent rocks?

After a few years, though, I began to see the joy of it. It is about the happenstance and randomness of finding such rocks. I don't mean to imply that there isn't some degree of strategy to it—there is indeed. After a friend held up a handful of bright orange rocks that looked like gems, I started to see the allure of recognizing these natural sweet colors along the riverscape. I'd seen them and found them before, but had never bent much of my will to it. After finding a couple of very nice ones, the size of my hand, I was soon turning my head to the gravel more and more when I'd pull over for a break while canoeing down the Willamette and other rivers.

For most people it seems just the pure gift of finding such a beautiful thing is enough. It is about what the river offers, and the sheer serendipity

This beautiful specimen was found on a gravel bar near Halsey, Oregon, after some high winter river flows.

of it. You can search endlessly for these river gifts and never find them. Freshly churned and morphed gravel bars that seem like they must contain many formerly submerged, vibrantly colored beauties may simply not have them. Methodically walking a pattern can work, yet often it does not work at all, and one's patience can be tested. If you are lucky, and you happen to be in a place that simply has that magic of the moment, they may well appear to you. That occurrence is the *river reveal*. At the same time, the whole engagement with the natural world of the river, agates or no agates, is the larger magic.

Traveling the side channel on that warm July day on the way to Hoacum Island Landing, Scott and I saw a nice assemblage of river life. Fish, mostly native, darted in the shallows, seemingly by the handfuls every meter. Native sculpin, suckers, shiners, sticklebacks, and trout abounded, both juveniles and adults. A few western pearlshell mussels could be seen in the first couple of miles of the channel, partially buried on the channel bottom, filtering the water as they held fast in the diminishing flow of summer.

Seeing the many species abounding in this shallow channel was somehow life-affirming. With so many things putting a challenge to this river, seemingly at every turn, here was this little side channel harboring all kinds of life native to the Willamette River; it provided a sense of hope. The native juga, the size of your fingernail and with a swirled black cone shell, hugged the rocks. Signs of beaver could be seen along the left bank, where numerous branches, devoid of bark, rested atop the silt or floated in the water. Clear markings stood out where the beaver's two front teeth had stripped the bark away and left long grooves in the moist pale-colored wood. Here and there small collections of floodplain forest hugged the channel, the cottonwood and ash providing shade, with occasional bunches of leafy willow and red osier dogwood clinging to the riparian fringe. All of this brought us a bit of optimism along this side channel, which held the hallmarks of a viable, even somewhat healthy, river system. It also made us think of what it might be like if there was a wider floodplain forest along both sides of the channel.

Not to revert to the negative after such hopeful observations, but we saw a few signs of trouble along this channel as well. It was clear that drainage into the channel from the surrounding fields was a daily occurrence: we saw multiple PVC pipes putting small streams of water back into the river system, all of it collected from the nearby fields where a likely network of underground conduits called "tiles" were collecting the irrigated flow. When vast expanses of fields employ artificial subsurface drainage conduits to move runoff toward the river, it is not a natural happening, and surely the system carries some measure of what is placed and sprayed on the fields directly into the main river and its tributaries. Along with the inputs of drainage from the fields, in some places the "strip" of riverside vegetation was very thin, or not present at all. These happenings were another sign of great human influence on this river. We also found a primitive effort to back up the channel with sandbags to enable irrigation water to be withdrawn—an easy-to-spot illegality.

At such points it is easy to see the problem, or at least a piece of it. People have had a very direct impact on this river for a very long time. If I had collected a sample of that river water along the side channel at Hoacum on that July morning, we could have screened it for myriad pollutants of different types. Looking at those samples with the best technology possible, sorting among the molecules composed of hydrogen and oxygen, a range of substances would have been found within. Based on recent experience, we would have identified nitrates, flame retardants, herbicides, and more. These pollutants, among others, have been found in this river system routinely. The findings matter because of the direct negative effects on the health of river species caused by these human-created toxic substances. It is another reminder of how much needs to be done for Oregon's green ways.

A quick jump out of the canoe, splashing along in the shallows over the gravels, then back in for a minute or two. Traveling like this in a canoe feels like the essence of summer. Feet wet, pulling the craft along a side channel with a couple of inches of water flowing over a gravel bar, then occasionally squeezing between the bank and a mess of large wood blocking the channel, then back into the boat was the travel mode for this side channel. These places remind me of walking the creeks of my suburban neighborhood when I was a kid. I sometimes laugh a bit, because as a middle-aged adult, I'm often doing the same kind of thing I was doing as a youth.

Splashing around in the water or walking quietly—the pattern was the same for me and others growing up. With some neighborhood kids, I would consistently turn my attention to the water. Risley Creek in Milwaukie was where I spent a lot of time from the ages of six to twelve, catching tadpoles and crayfish all the way, stepping ever so carefully amid the dark rocks of the creek, being vigilant to not step into a hole or some deep spot that would immerse me just a bit too much. Splashing though was just part of the program, and we did that aplenty. My travels along the beautiful Willamette side channels seem one and the same. This kind of exploration is just as fun for me as a middle-aged person as it was in my youth.

When I paddle and explore the river, some of that same feeling—the element of the beauty, and of the unknown—is revealed any time I'm on the water or riverside lands. Even in areas I frequent along the river, each trip can be different from the one before. Subtleties of vegetation, river flow, the presence of wildlife and the angle of light change from day to day. One day the riverside floodplain is rich with green willow and ash, yet sparked with little else. Only a few days later, the water of the main river continues to drop, revealing new gravel bars, and the same floodplain lands are interspersed with the pink blooms of Nootka rose, or Douglas spirea. The angle and warmth of the sunlight squeezing through the lush riverside vegetation can morph from moment to moment, and from day to day.

Traveling along the side channel at Hoacum, after a while you reach the thinnest line of land separating the side channel from the main river. Though it is not visible from the side channel (and on private land), if you could rise up about twenty feet you would see the main channel of the Willamette only fifteen yards from the side channel and, at the top of the thin string of land separating the two flows, a one-lane road. In the old days the river had likely pulsed through this thin bit of land, with much of the main channel making its way down what is today the side channel. This reality seems evident from USGS photos from the 1950s, and from maps from 1894 and before. At some point, the river reverted back to the eastern channel, today's mainstem Willamette.

Change and its inevitability are felt in these places. On one side of the thin line of soil and rock is a big, high-volume floodplain river, separated from a small sinewy side channel on the other. The present-day separation is enabled by large riprap rocks placed on the mainstem bank by the private landowner, along with some of the retired rails from the local railroad, arranged in a fashion to create a kind of steel frame to hold the rock in place. In this case, the landowner was seeking to preserve road access to his agricultural land. The structure stretches along the outside bend for a couple of hundred yards. In just a few years, some of the rock has already been stripped away by high water. Even though it is a lot of steel and rock, it still feels pretty temporary. Recently this landowner sold out to an out-of-state corporation — one transitioning the property to hazelnut growing, and its related soil regime that is seemingly cleared of all living things to aid in the collection of the nuts during harvest. Given the pace and scope of this new surge in the transition to hazelnuts around the Willamette Valley, practices employed on these orchards merit a closer look and ongoing evaluation.

Someday the main river will likely push through this thin man-made bit of land, to again fuel the side channel with water volume similar to the main channel, for a time at least. Here the landowner's efforts will likely succumb to the power of the water. When I look back a few years, I honestly can't recall how this project was ever approved by NOAA Fisheries and the US Army Corps of Engineers. The river always wins this kind of competition — it is simply just a matter of time. Similar efforts by

Some mature Willamette
Valley pines are found
on this little Greenway
outpost at Hoacum Island.

landowners are visible all along the Willamette, with human willpower
exerted against the mass of the river's working water. Endless pulsing and
erosive events eventually erode the river's banks, slice by slice or in a few
big shoves. Broad and sporadic, the water continues to work. Yet, from
south to north, expanses of large rocks coat the riverbank, and in places
dark wood pilings are sunk into the river's edge at the top of the coating of
rock. Even today, people still work to tame the river.

   When my friend Scott and I jumped back into the canoe after walking over a gravel bar, we found a bit of current and squeezed the canoe
between a big root mass and part of a cottonwood tree trunk. What was
unusual about this trip is that I was in the bow of the canoe. Usually I
paddle in the stern, because the canoe I typically use is my own. Thankfully though, on this day I was in the bow of Scott's canoe. Scott had
always had awesome luck finding agates and had quite a collection at

home—he was one of the main instigators of my interest in agates. We paddled onward, talking. As we rounded the bend on the small channel, my eyes were drawn to the shoreline just a few feet ahead of us. I may have uttered an expletive of some sort, and I pointed to it. "Whoooaa man, looook at thaaaat!" There in front of us was the biggest agate we had ever seen on the river.

I hopped out of the boat, and Scott saw it too. "Ohhh myyy gaawwwd, look at that," he said in his slight Georgia accent. I walked the few feet to where the agate rested along the shoreline and picked it up. Partially wet from the water, the whole rock glowed a kind of brilliant orange and white. Clear veins of orange coursed through the rock, interspersed with a semitranslucent white—it was something out of this world. I placed it back on the bank and took a photo. Contrasting against the dark rock of the shoreline, the orange and white agate radiated light. I considered leaving it where it was, but in the end I picked it up and placed it into the canoe.

Scott was just shaking his head the whole time. "Today, it's like one out of twenty times you are in the bow of any canoe," he said, laughing and shaking his head. He had never seen anything like it either in his many days traveling the river. The agate measures about eight inches by nine inches—not an oval or perfect circle, but instead sort of an irregular and beautiful mass born of pressure, heat, chemistry, and time. Serendipity was the only word that came to mind upon the happenstance of seeing this orange thing along the river. Of all the chances that the big rock would be uncovered, and then to have a river traveler come by at just the right moment—and on a side channel. It could have just as easily fallen into one of the few deep pools along that side channel, and yet it did not. We muttered about this rock for a long time after, and still do.

After an hour and a half of paddling and shuffling through the shallows every so often along the Hoacum side channel, exhilarated by what the river had provided in the agate, along with everything else, we reached the swath of green of Hoacum Island Landing. We returned to the canoe, paddling a bit downstream, where the broad-stemmed and leafed reed canary grass coated the shoreline when we nudged the canoe inland shortly after. There was little to rope the canoe to, so we hefted it up and over the bright green grass; where the hull of the crimson-colored craft nestled downward, the long grass reached up and over the canoe's gunnels, holding it in place. There was no game trail, so we just pressed inward amid the tall grass, carefully walking up through the invasive expanse. All the while our careful steps tested for the solidness of the ground beneath, neither of us wanting to drop into a hole. Soon the grass thinned, and we reached a band of willow. As soon as we reached the willows, we could see an open expanse on the inland side beyond. We pressed through the rich line of willow to reach the floodplain meadow. I was immediately struck by this place. It was strange in some way, right off the bat. I wondered how this particular parcel had been obtained by the State of Oregon and what, if anything, had ever been done here. Had it been farmed or used for agriculture at some point? That occurrence was common to many Greenway sites.

Wild onion dotted the expanse of dry, well-drained, rocky soil. The day was hot for the valley, perhaps 85 degrees, and the open area spread out for perhaps twenty-five acres before it met a band of trees and shrubs on the eastern border of the property. Hoacum is situated at an inside bend of the side channel, with an open meadow on the west side of the roughly half oval property and a forest tract of approximately twenty acres to the east. Tilled fields rub against the forest at the property line. The contrast is sharp between the public ownership to the west and the private ownership to the east.

Hoacum clocks in at only about forty acres total, but it seems that isolation from the mainstem Willamette, and its existence as an island of "natural" in the middle of vast tracts of cultivated land, lend the property some distinction. Years before the visit on this summer day, I had visited Hoacum on a cool overcast spring afternoon, again with Scott. We had sought the property, as on this day, to reach it and explore it a bit. Unfortunately, on that day it was a short trip. We had paddled in as far as we could from the downstream end. We waded through the shallows, at one point up to our chests in water. After a time, we made it through the riparian zone and into the forest on the north side. We had just hoped to get there, take a look at things, and return after about an hour.

As we pushed our way into the riparian forest, I recall looking down to my hand after feeling something crawling on it as we were scanning the tree canopy for birds. Usually feeling something crawling its way along your hand is no big deal—perhaps a spider, maybe a cricket, a bumblebee, or a leech. I looked down to see which it was. Instead I saw a large black wasp. In what seemed an instantaneous burst, I shook it off—and in a simultaneous confirmation I felt the sharp pain where it had just stung me. Two or three more wasps buzzed us, and in a flash we burst out of the riparian zone, leaping over the grass and through brambles toward the side channel.

Outward into the air from the top of the bank I went, with Scott not far behind. The telltale buzzing of the wasps could still be heard in pursuit. Supernaturally charged with the burst of adrenaline, or so it felt, I leaped toward the water and descended through the air, all the while my arms up and legs extended. Here the side channel was usually fairly shallow, but with the amount of water from the spring flows the channel was at least up to our necks in places. In a moment I hit the water, managing to stay upright, all the while holding my camera as high as possible where I grasped it in my right hand. Scott whisked down the bank and we turned to look back from where we had come, carefully walking in the channel, hoping to not hit a hole that would send us swimming. Here and there the dark wasps whirred in the air above the bank, but none seemed to be following us. "Shit I think we bumped right into the hive," said Scott. "It was right there on a low branch." We both watched and waiting for another minute or two, as I watched my skin react to where the wasp had punctured me. I had not even seen the nest.

You feel that peculiar physical rush, being pursued by some form of wildlife, feeling that tinge of adrenaline jump into your system. Even when you know your life is not necessarily in danger, or so you think, that surge is surprising. A simultaneous thought seems to occur in tandem with the reassuring one that you likely will not die—but that other thought is right there. In this case it was that perhaps my body's response to multiple wasp stings had never been tested, let alone against what might have been a whole hive's worth.

This time, glancing back to the open meadow, I could see that strip of forest we had visited before, and I wished we had made it to this point on the earlier trip. Thanks to the wasp, that trip had been abbreviated, and we had gained only the briefest glimpse of Hoacum that day. We walked out into the open. Here the soil was thin and very dry, with occasional rocks showing through. It had the feel of some kind of old-time riverside prairie habitat of the Willamette Valley lowlands. Certainly we could go no lower than this riverside lowland. Untouched was a word that came to mind that day—which is unusual for the riverside lands. Nothing seems to have gone on here in a long while—no cultivation (if ever), no visitation (no tracks other than those from the resident deer and other wildlife), and a feel of quiet, even though we were hemmed in by agricultural land. In one spot, it appeared someone had taken a bit of gravel out in a slight, small depression years back, but that was it. The whirr of crickets, the whisp of the afternoon wind through the skyward cottonwoods—these were the sounds of Hoacum Island Landing.

Over the hours we were there, I detected other sounds: in the distance the hum of farm machinery, an airplane here and there, and a truck on the gravel road across the adjacent field. Yet the foreground of my riverside soundscape was the flow of the current around the property and the working of the bees gently rising and lowering amid the riparian fringe, wholly immersed in the world of flowers and pollination, with the heat radiating from the floodplain crust. Here and there dragonflies and damselflies—brilliant with their energy and quick flight—traveled past, moving on to the next patch of wild-garlic-covered earth. My feeling here, having expended some effort to reach it, was that this slice of land, this little green oasis, had been largely forgotten. I pondered that idea, a small fragment of land, worked by the power of the river for centuries, yet perhaps pretty much unknown. A feeling crept into me, as it has before, that these small parcels have been better left forgotten.

Scott walked ahead across the field, then stopped. "Ceanothus," he said, pointing to the dark green bushes in the middle of the relatively arid field. Ceanothus is a plant more attuned to the drier slopes, and it was uncommon in the valley, let alone in the middle of the floodplain. It was one of several signals that told us this place was unique. The solid presence of poison oak was also something to be watchful for as we walked.

A couple of years after this visit, we returned with an expert botanist working on a contract for Oregon Parks on a summer project to catalog the botanical riches of their properties. We made the effort to get him to Hoacum, this time part way up the lower stretch of the side channel in July by powerboat, then walking in the rest of the way. A local landowner had allowed passage across a slice of their land to get to the property. As we entered the property, almost immediately the botanist stopped and knelt to the ground, looking at a flower, "Navarretia," he said. Although this plant could be purchased from a nursery, it was native and pretty rare in the floodplain. We continued on, finding more flowers that were not frequently seen in native floodplain habitat. "Turkey mullein," the botanist said, again surprised at the find. "There is stuff here that I've only seen in the Willamette Valley a handful to times in my years doing this work," he said. We continued in this fashion for a couple of hours, with the botanist stopping, looking, and shaking his head at the wonder around us. "Another native grass, in this case Lemmon's needlegrass," he said. "Bottlebrush squirreltail, Oregon golden aster, barestem buckwheat [*Eriogonum nudum*], Roemer's fescue, Piper's willow—wow, by far the best native prairie remnant I've seen," he remarked.

As we completed our reconnaissance, a question was at hand: What made this place different from some of the other Greenway parcels along the Willamette? I had a suspicion, as did Scott. I returned home that night and dove into some old maps of the Willamette. After a bit, I found the map I was looking for. An early US Army Corps of Engineers survey map from 1894 shows the main channel of the river moving through what is today's somewhat more slender-cut side channel, but more importantly, it showed the side channel around Hoacum Island being a much larger channel. The Army Corps maps from this period are pretty interesting, showing hand-drawn shapes of the landscape, with symbols reflecting the occasional farmhouse, orchard, and riverside forest. In some places there is a short description, such as "thick brush and cottonwood forest." I looked hard at this map and was astonished to see the Hoacum Island Greenway property reflected there. I recognized it immediately. To confirm, I quickly pulled up a current-day aerial photo and arranged it next to the map from the late 1800s. Our suspicions were confirmed: the property was basically exactly the same on both images.

Rounding toward the west, the channel shape was more or less the same, the open field mimicking what was there 125 years back, and the fringe of trees was the same. The main difference was that the forest continued to the east across the floodplain, where today there is a large open field. The reality was quite simple: this area had never been cultivated, built on, or otherwise disturbed by people. Likely this was because the open area was poor soil for agriculture, given its low elevation and many rocks—likely it was once the river bottom for part of the year.

Examples such as Hoacum are somewhat rare on the Willamette; a few other properties have similar attributes, having been left alone amid

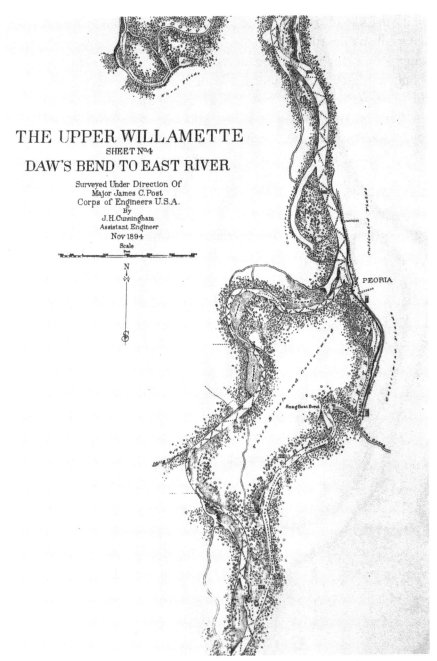

THE UPPER WILLAMETTE
SHEET No4
DAW'S BEND TO EAST RIVER

Surveyed Under Direction Of
Major James C. Post
Corps of Engineers U.S.A.
By
J.H.Cunningham
Assistant Engineer
Nov 1894
Scale

The old US Army Corps map of Hoacum Island from 1894. The area of today's Hoacum Island Landing appears much the same on the old map.

all the decades of activity around them. At Hoacum Island Greenway, the old seedbank was still there in the soil, still generating native wildflowers among the many nonnative plants and invasive plants—which we also found on Hoacum. Such property along the river is pretty unique. I sent the side-by-side images to Scott, and he agreed with the assessment.

I'm a bit torn about even writing about this wonderful place. At the same time, it is not easy to get to, and is full of poison oak—as such sites often are, which is problematic for some folks. I have to believe that the person seeking to make the trip would have the best of intentions—looking only for the peace and solitude of the natural area. It also seems to me that writing about this mostly hidden beauty can inspire more effort into protecting and restoring other public lands along the river.

8
The Three Greens

> Those who contemplate the beauty of the earth find reserves of
> strength that will endure as long as life lasts. There is something
> infinitely healing in the repeated refrains of nature — the assurance that
> dawn comes after night, and spring after winter.
>
> —Rachel Carson, *Silent Spring*

For folks who live in the Corvallis and Albany areas, an assemblage of
beautiful properties can be found just a few miles downstream or up from
the centers of these towns: Half Moon Bend, Riverside Landing, and
Tripp Island. Truax Island Greenway is also just upstream of the others
but is difficult to access from the river.

Each of these properties has its own story to tell. Here and there the
floodplain forest is deep and rich. Half Moon Bend comes first: a couple
hundred acres, with a rich forest as well as a wide-open area. Over the
years I've seen and heard great horned owls on this property, and at one
time encountered a large nest on the northern flank of the open interior, in an old cottonwood. Over the last decade, effort has been made to
replant the open meadow of the interior. Today this area supports many
native plants that are growing and thriving. At the same time, this property
is frequently visited by people on quad wheelers, which are illegal at Half
Moon. Sometimes local folks act to the detriment of a property that is
better suited to quiet, low-impact use.

Riverside Landing is next as you head downriver. Its couple hundred acres meshes with private land in a conservation easement to the
north and east, making a nice complex of native habitat, and areas that
will be further restored. Riverside Landing is quiet, with much area that
can be explored. I've camped along the shore here a couple of times
over the years and made forays inland to seek out birds and backwaters.
It has no developed trails, so you just have to seek out the deer trails

and open areas. Floodplain forest reveals all manner of native plants and animals.

In 2010, Bennett Hall, a reporter from the *Corvallis Gazette-Times*, as well as photographer Mark Ylen, joined me for a half-day canoe trip from Corvallis to Albany to visit a couple of Greenway properties and to talk about the river generally. Bennett wanted to see the Greenway and learn a bit about the program, as well as recreational opportunities along the river in that area. Of course, pollution was always a topic of interest, especially comparing the historic issues with current-day issues.

The two of them were eager to get out there, and the photographer, Mark, had brought his own recreational kayak. Mark had his cameras and lenses in the bottom of the kayak between his legs, in a dry bag. Bennett and I paddled a canoe. What was unusual about this particular paddle trip was that the water was exceedingly high for late spring—I had reservations about the effort and thought perhaps we should postpone it. But of course it was a beautiful May morning, and the sun seems to have had an influence on our thinking, even though the river was high and brown. In just a few minutes we were whisked downriver by the big flow. It was certainly not the largest volume I'd paddled on the Willamette, but it was a lot of water all the same. I was most concerned with the photographer, but after a few minutes it looked like he would do just fine, barring some major mistake. The intent of the excursion was to show them Half Moon Bend, Riverside Landing, and Tripp Island—all OPRD Greenway properties. We also wanted to discuss the need for habitat restoration and the acquisition of more riverside public land.

After a brief stop at Half Moon Bend, we continued on to Riverside Landing. It was hummocky, with a low bank in some places and a few feet of bank in others; we landed our craft and walked a bit inland with the intention of looking around a bit. Replete with Oregon ash, willow, cottonwood, and other native forest species, the property was gorgeous. The timing was nearly perfect to get a sense of how floodplains work. Here and there water flowed across the property because of the high river flows. Small creek-sized flows pushed across the gravels and newly leafed-out willows.

It was great to see a simple expedition to explore the Greenway work out, and also great that a local reporter was interested in the topic at hand. Over the years I'd seen and experienced a lot of people who "worked" on

This awesome black cottonwood at Riverside Landing stands tall in the early summer sun.

Willamette issues, their professional lives helping dictate what policies and rules were put forward concerning the river. It was, and is, always interesting to me, though, that some of them had scarcely visited the river or its tributaries. That has always seemed like an oddity to me. Certainly, some of these people made a point of spending professional and personal time along the river, but plenty do not. Over the years I've worked to remedy this situation.

Having had a small stable of canoes for my job, and a couple personally, it has been my goal to have people use them on trips, whether organized outings on a particular stretch of river or an expedition tailored to a specific person or need. Loaning out a personal canoe to those taking a weekend day or two to explore a stretch of the Willamette has also been commonplace. Canoes and related paddle craft are basically pointless if they are not being used regularly. It was refreshing to have Bennett and Mark along, with both so enthusiastic about getting on the water.

We made our way into the property and quickly encountered water moving in from upstream—a side channel had recently been reborn! It was not unusual to see this with higher flows, but often access could be an issue. Here the three of us were witnessing the river "doing its thing," as Stan Gregory—a prominent, well-known fisheries biologist who has added considerable knowledge to the world about the Willamette and how it functions—has observed more than once. During his years at Oregon State University he, along with his awesome colleague Randy Wildman, has provided essential data on a range of species and helped to elevate awareness of the need for more healthy floodplain habitat along the river.

Water coursed across the gravel, flowing along the contours of the gravel bar and snaking inland. At one point we pushed slowly forward and had to cross a flow that had already reached a couple of feet in depth. We were careful to not step into a deeper depression in the gravel as we brushed by willows, ash, and snowberry. Not wanting to tempt fate, we turned back toward our canoe and kayak, just in case the water continued to rise, though the forecast that morning had predicted that the levels would stay relatively constant.

Witnessing the growing channels made the notion of properly functioning floodplains very easy to see and understand. I could imagine a range of species taking the opportunity to move their way inland, for a time, then following the water back out. Other species would benefit from the influx of water into backwater areas that remained pooled up throughout the summer. Instead of drying out, the deeply shaded backwater in some areas can be routinely recharged by high winter and spring flows, benefiting western pond turtles and myriad other critters. This was Exhibit A that Bennett and Mark were able to take away from our adventure.

Tripp Island was next, just downriver from Riverside Landing. Over the years this island has grown in size. Typically, by mid- to late July the side channel is nearly depleted of water, but before then a person can usually guide a canoe or kayak down the little channel. Some years the channel dries up completely, as it did in 2017. Like the other two properties, this Greenway site is often quiet and beautiful, though smaller than Half Moon or Riverside Landing. Tripp is about twenty acres, but it contains a nice little floodplain forest and an expanse of small gravels. To the west is a gravel quarry with intermittent activity, which can be problematic for peace and quiet along the river.

After our exploration of Riverside Landing, the three of us headed past Tripp Island, and, with the fast current, we were soon at Hyak Park, the end point of our paddle. Bennett and Mark left with a much fuller understanding of the Greenway lands along that stretch of the Willamette, and how they benefit wildlife and people.

At Tripp Island one previous April day, I had walked the island with some friends. We had decided to make camp on the island, and after setting our tents up, we explored. Newly emerged cottonwood and willow leaves were soaking up the sun to the west. The side channel was full and deep, with fast water that carried with it the wintry cold from high in the mountains. Here the gravel is marvelous. Over the years the island has morphed quite a bit as the river's currents have moved gravel around. Large flows have also brought in new gravels from upstream. A wonderful analysis of this change has been captured by ecologist Patricia Benner. Benner's analysis, using historical aerial photos of the island, shows a small gravel bar growing remarkably, over the years, into today's relatively stable island. I think I first heard Patricia say it, but the island is indeed "agate island." Like many other areas of the river, the island's smaller rocks get moved and remixed by high flows. After the water recedes, a relatively new palette can be exposed to explore, with the receding flows revealing occasional deeply colored gems. Combined with sunlight and the emerging beauty of the spring bloom, it can feel like the perfect place to spend time.

On that same April escapade, western pearlshell mussels were a feature of our experience. Toward the bottom end of the side channel, we had made our way during an afternoon walk. Vibrant willow shoots were everywhere radiating their newly green beauty. Over the course of the winter the high flows had created depressions in the gravel bar, essentially circular and oval bowls in the gravel. Some of these were several meters across and a few feet deep in places, excavated by strong current. In a couple of these unique depressions we found the familiar elongated dark oval shells of western pearlshell mussels. Wading into the water we picked them up—indeed they were live mussels. The pool in this case was just a few meters from the side channel. High spring and winter flows had likely pushed them downstream from mussel beds a short distance upstream on the main river. In times of extraordinary flows, even these relatively heavy, adult hand-sized creatures could be moved downstream with some regularity. Most of the mussels we saw that day were fairly large, and assumed to be adults.

In a few places we could see the telltale trail of where a mussel had moved itself from the receding water of the bowl to the receding water of the side channel. Other lines could be seen heading into the deeper portions of the bowl. Shallow grooves or deep lines in the small gravels and sediment of Tripp Island showed the path of individual mussels. It always amazes me to see these "mussel trails." To think that this creature managed to push itself across the gravel with its fleshy foot—millimeter by millimeter, to the water of the side channel in order to stay alive. Over hours the mussel must have slowly made its way, all the while somehow avoiding being trapped by some unknown obstacle or consumed by a predator. Without sight, hearing, or a sense of smell as we know it, these mollusks can sense the diminished level of the water and seek to find a way to survive in the nearby flow. Given the physics of the river's flow, the river rock bowls would become shallow and stagnant, if not completely depleted of water, long before the side channel would. It was easy to see the predicament for them on this sunny spring day. Soon, the pool would be no more, and the native creatures that could live longer than most humans would eventually expire in an isolated dry depression on the gravel island.

I'm not sure who said it first, but one of us uttered, "Let's move them." It was a quick, unanimous agreement. Over about a half hour, we identified a couple dozen mussels in that pool and another nearby, and we moved them all into the depth of the nearby side channel's lowest portion, which typically stayed wet in the hot months. We could only wade a little over a foot, not wanting to overtop our boots. Our booted feet entered the Willamette flow, deeply chilled by the mountain snows. Carefully leaning forward, we plunged our hands into the water, seeking to orient the mussels in the deepest flows we could reach. Given our limitations in equipment, we gently tossed many toward the deepest water. It was a simple exercise of having few options but hoping for the best outcome for these creatures.

Tripp is a small place but full of bird life, beaver, and other elements of nature. The tell-tale signs of beaver along the shoreline—small willow shoots shorn of bark—were abundant. Beaver, the state animal of Oregon, is a relatively understudied creature. Ironically, the state invests very little in seeking to understand their general health and abundance. Given what they provide to the riverine ecosystem, it would seem more should be done for beavers. Even in the current day, beaver are considered a "nuisance" animal by the state, and are far too easy to trap and kill. Recent legislative bills designed to better understand and protect this foundational species have been brought to the Oregon legislature, but none have gained even a hearing. This truly pathetic political outcome speaks volumes about keeping certain interests happy and free of regulation. It makes little sense to trap, harass, or kill such a cool animal that also helps create ecological complexity along our rivers and that, in higher elevations, can help reduce the spread of wildfire. In coming years, the many people who love these riverine, lake, and creek-loving rodents will win out by creating better protections for this wonderful species. The original white trappers came to Oregon to trap beaver, in the process nearly wiping them out in some river systems, but perhaps now we can turn the tide and do more for conservation and direct protection for this important species in the coming years.

Tripp Island is a place of rest, natural beauty, and relaxation. That is one of the things that burned in my brain one Fourth of July on this beautiful Greenway island not that long ago. You see, I was camped with friends and family on the lower portion of the property, on a large gravel bar just across from the downstream end of the island, still part of the public's ownership. The upper campsite on the island was occupied by other campers—a couple of power boats of people had been there for a day or two, so we chose the downstream site.

The day had been sunny, with osprey filling they sky. Swainson's thrushes called from the forest behind our camp, with the gentle summer wind carrying their songs across the water. As evening arrived, the sense of peace pervaded throughout our camp. Then, all of us nearly jumped out of our camp chairs as a massive boom shook the area! Yes indeed, it was clearly a very large firecracker, akin to the M-80 explosives of earlier times. Then, as we all sought to figure out whether someone was lighting these things on land, or elsewhere, another giant boom went off. In essence, these were half sticks of dynamite that drowned out any sense of calm that we had—erasing the peace of the place immediately. I've always thought these creations are beyond stupid, outside of more formal celebrations.

It is one thing to deal fairly with an issue, and another to do so with a tinge of anger. It was clear to all of us that the people camping on the top end of the island were the source. We clearly had different values for being in such a place, to say the least. All of us in our group believe in freedom, and freewill, yet there is a time and place for everything, and to us, even on the Fourth of July, lighting massive firecrackers off in a natural area was the absolute wrong move.

In a minute I threw on my PFD, grabbed a paddle, and jumped into my empty canoe. Soon I was across the channel and pulled the craft onto the rocks. I walked for a couple of minutes across the gravels of the island heading in the upstream direction, through the expanse of willows that blocked the other camp from view. After a minute I could view their tents. A few people looked my way from about a hundred meters, and in a moment half the group receded into their tents, or to the shoreline, away from what appeared to be the main person in camp—one of the camp elders, so to speak. He looked to be in his late fifties, and a younger guy was next to him. It seemed these may well be the "celebrators." I walked up close to both of them. I then introduced myself.

"Did you light that M-80 off?" The older of the two looked at me, then away. The two of them were looking at the ground, then me briefly, and then back to the ground. "Uh, yeah, that was us."

Inside I was quite annoyed but worked to remain calm and collected as I talked with them. There are a lot of things to be angry about regarding the Willamette—this was just another in a long line. What is hard for me to understand though is that, in a place more or less ready-made to provide a bit of an escape from the noise of the city, nearby traffic, construction, and more, here these folks were in a beautiful quiet setting on the Willamette Greenway seeking to celebrate Independence Day by making as much noise as humanly possible. It was no mere series of firecrackers. They were playing with something much larger.

"Well gentlemen, you should know that, first of all, lighting that mini-bomb off here is simply unwise, and not in keeping with Greenway natural areas—or the value that most of us place in being out here. These places are not for that kind of activity. Further, what you are doing is illegal on land owned on the Greenway by Oregon State Parks," I said. The two of them looked at the ground and said they were sorry and would not do it again. I could not help a final comment. "If I hear another one of those, or anything like it, you will not like the result. The river rangers around here don't look kindly on this type of thing." They apologized again and turned away. I chuckled to myself on the walk back to the canoe. Somehow the image of the "Rangers of Central Park" in the movie *Elf* popped into my head. I know that my friend Scott, who used to be a river ranger, often wished that he could exercise a bit more robust authority on behalf of the public along the Greenway, but that is another story.

Of course the world is full of larger problems that need attention, for sure, and no person is perfect. I certainly don't hold myself to that standard, and I'd fail if I did. In this case, though, I had the distinct sense that this type of action, this little-considered deed by these folks camping along the river was in some way in keeping with the wider world of ill-conceived actions conducted every day by people, and by our society. The line between right and wrong, the weave of ethics and baseline conduct that many people learn in life seems to be a bit more tattered than it used to be. Hopefully that group had a chance to think on the issue and perhaps even agree that, on the public lands they were using, the sound of a nighthawk at dusk flying over the river and the peace of their campfire were more important aspects of celebrating than lighting off small sticks of dynamite.

I made my way back to camp and the rest of our night was peaceful as we enjoyed the colors of a glorious sunset, and then a sky that was soon awash with a slice of the cosmos. Now that is more fitting along the riverscape, even during the Fourth of July.

If you explore any of these properties, you may well notice something about the surrounding land use. Each of these properties has a fair amount of gravel. As a consequence, and as on other parts of the river, gravel extraction represents a significant use of the landscape. Given the river's historic carving and meandering, along with the flush of rock large and small from upstream to down, much of the floodplain is composed of large deposits of river rock, easily evident in many areas by taking a simple stroll along the water and then inland. Generally the deposits are very deep in the southern stretch of the river and slowly become more shallow as one moves northward. Deposits more than a hundred feet deep in Eugene become shallower in the mid-valley and below. In either instance, gravel extraction has been, and remains, a significant resource extraction activity whether one is in Eugene or north of Salem. From this raw material, concrete is produced, as well as other "rock" products.

Over the years this industry has been the focus of significant discussion. To what degree do large open pits adjacent to the river, the result of mining, affect water quality? Do large open water bodies, typically left after mining has occurred, become breeding grounds for invasive fish if they

A natural depression in the rock after high flows have scoured out a portion of the gravel bar.

are opened up to the main channel, resulting in a detrimental impact to wild salmon? Can these large open pits be captured by the river at flood, and how much do they affect the flow and quality of groundwater? Other questions also arise in relation to gravel mining, from impacts to water quality during mining to the overall aesthetic of noise and dust so close to private and public lands—especially a public waterway that people seek out for some degree of quiet and solitude.

What we witness too often today are large pits full of water, when active mining ceases—in essence artificial lakes adjacent to the river in many areas. They are steep at the edge, typically holding water that is warmer than the river, and can become breeding grounds for fish that might eat juvenile salmon. In some cases, there is a worry of "pit recapture" caused by high flood flows. In such a case, the Willamette would rise to the point where it could modify the gravel pit walls and enable the open pit to connect to the Willamette. This notion is particularly evident at the Willamette McKenzie confluence, where large pits nearly surround the confluence area. Looking at some Willamette aerial photographs, one is hard pressed to see the river in this stretch.

It is likely that the original notion of the Greenway did not envision massive gravel extraction operations adjacent to the relatively scant, few hundred acres of public Greenway lands at certain locations along the river. This is the case at Tripp Island for sure. It is somewhat ironic that some vibrant, gorgeous tree-coated public properties are subject to the constant sounds of mining equipment creaking along the floodplain nearby. At times the audio assault can be daunting, with the incessant sound of trucks backing up, beeping almost continuously, and the rumblings of processing machinery in the distance. Behind that incursion on one's senses, the low grumble of machinery digging into the earth to scrape away the gravel deposits is ever present.

Not long ago I spoke with a person affiliated with a family-owned gravel company, and he said a new mining area would take the sound issue seriously. Instead of loud beeping when the trucks back up, there would be the low sound of a duck quacking. It was hard to believe, but a lovely concept. Progress!

For some folks in the agricultural sector in the Willamette Valley, the thought of mining operations rankles them even more than conserving land for nature. This is because, typically, the upper layer of floodplain land is prime agricultural soil—with layer upon layer of silt having been deposited by high flows over many years. In order to get to some gravel deposits, that topsoil must be removed. In doing so, the "prime farmland," as it is referred to by some, is dramatically altered. While it is valid to debate whether farming operations should operate so very close to the river in many places, the irritation felt by some agricultural folks toward the gravel mining industry is easily seen—and at times seems pretty ironic.

The notion that "you cannot take farmland out of production," has been repeated likely thousands of times over the decades by some folks. Some agricultural lobbyists continue to express similar sentiments, whether the idea is to restore floodplain lands to better enable the river to function naturally or to permit another proposed gravel extraction operation along the river; as you might guess, there is a pretty clear distinction between these two types of land use. One can also argue that all three uses—gravel extraction, farming, and restoration—provide some clear societal benefits. We need rock for roads, foundations for houses and buildings, and more; it is made into concrete and other materials, which do not magically appear from thin air. We also need food—though of course a large percentage of Willamette Valley agriculture has been devoted to grass seed production for decades, instead of vegetables and grains. At the same time having natural landscapes that can filter runoff, provide habitat, absorb high flows, and much more provides a very necessary ecological service—a service that also has a huge economic value. Natural ecological production is a real thing.

The "out of production" notion seems vastly overused and, frankly, overstates the "value" of said land use. If you fly at low elevation over the Willamette River, or simply view an online aerial photograph, it is easy to see there is absolutely no lack of agricultural land in the Willamette Valley. In fact, it would make sense to start up a new phrase, in many instances: "We need to bring our floodplains (riverlands) back into *natural* production." From the air the issue is easy to see. Our natural systems have suffered greatly because they have been destroyed. We need to restore thousands of acres of floodplain lands in systems like the Willamette to restore threatened species, to increase clean water, to increase the ability of the riverland to limit the destruction of floods, and to provide people with more access to nature. This value-added aspect of restoration has been well documented by numerous economic analyses over the years.

Restoration is part of giving back something to the natural world that was taken many years ago. When you rob a river of its natural function, you are taking from each and every species that relies on the river and its function for survival—from salmon and osprey to western pond turtles and green heron to the tiny native sculpin and freshwater mussel. If one views what the natural ecological function provides in economic terms, and in helping to curb flooding, the equation easily pencils out against growing crops in terms of flood damage alone.

This is not to say that agriculture should stop. Not at all. It is to say that, in some places, the use can, and should, change, for the benefit of water quality, flood control, habitat value, and recreational value. It is really about healthy ecosystems and biodiversity. In this vein, it makes sense to change ownership of the river's floodplain, adding back to public ownership a few thousand acres over the next two decades. Further, such habitat

A common sight—gravel pits large and small along the river from Eugene to Newberg.

can help provide resiliency in the face of climate change. This ownership change would add thousands of acres of land that, rather than producing grass seed, a growing mass of hazelnuts, and the chemical by-products of both enterprises, could instead produce huge ecological benefits.

The Oregon Department of Geology and Mineral Industries (DOGAMI) has regulated and currently administers the permit process for new gravel pits, as well as the day-to-day operation of these extraction sites. Few would fight the notion that, historically, the level of regulation has been weak at best, and gravel extraction operations have had a very tight grip on DOGAMI, the agency that regulates them. One might envision that the gray of the river rock extraction process has had very little to do with anything that is inherently green. Issues related to floodplain health, river recapture of pits, wastewater generated by these operations, the noise of day-to-day operations—one can argue that for decades the green ways of this industry have been virtually nonexistent. One might submit that Oregon's regulatory structure has been weak at best in regard to gravel mining in the floodplain. Thankfully, there has been some new thinking at this agency.

In recent years there has been more movement to reconnect mined-out gravel pits to the benefit of the river — if the conditions are right. Among those in the gravel industry I've spoken with over the years, there is clearly growing interest in doing something right for the river. Some good plans have come from Wilsonville Concrete, with a smaller planned operation on Grand Island below Salem, that would leave their site in better ecological condition than what has been done there for generations. Some experimentation related to topsoil has also been done with the much larger Knife River operation near Corvallis, as well as experiments with creating off-channel habitat. Pits that are more shallow provide better opportunities for reconnection to the main river, or for habitat restoration, given their similarity to natural river depths. It is intuitive really: shallower pits mimic more natural river conditions, and as a consequence, modification to a more natural shape and aspect is much easier with a fifteen-foot pit than with fifty-foot or greater depth pit. Gravel pits surrounding the river in the Eugene area are some that will be exceedingly difficult to conduct restoration activities with, given their significant depth.

In the first few years of the 2000s, an operator or two began to think more broadly about the impact of their activities. They questioned how they could return some of the topsoil best-suited to agriculture to former mine sites that had been exhausted of gravel. Others wondered how they could configure their gravel extraction pattern and overall footprint on the land to better enable habitat restoration at the end of mining. This type of thinking occurred with a smaller, more nimble company that seemed to truly care about their impact in the floodplain. Given the length of the typical mining permit and overall operation, it will be at least a couple of decades before we see how firmly their commitment remains.

As the years have gone by, DOGAMI has begun to recognize that their historic regulatory framework had to change, and over the past few years the department has taken steps to better regulate and enforce permits, and to think of the final footprint of mined-out sites that would not be seen for decades down the road, given the long lifespan of mining permits in Oregon. As it now stands, the gravel pit to the west of Tripp Island has opened up again in earnest. At present there seem to be no limits on the gravel quarry's operations to reduce impacts to those recreating peacefully along the river.

9
The Willamette Mission

> Long ago only Indians lived in this country. They did not labor so as to
> find their food. It merely grew on the prairies, in the hills.
>
> —William Hartless, Kalapuya tribal member, quoted
> in "The Kalapuyans" from Chris Mercier

Some places along the Willamette River are resonant with multiple generations of connection and conflict. Some locations along the river also
reflect the level of aspiration that can be found in recent years regarding
the river's health. Some places represent both. It seems to me that the
general area of today's Mission Bottom area stands out, for being the site
of some interesting moments in Oregon history and at the same time
drawing a clear line to what is possible for a healthy, naturally functioning
river system. The Willamette Mission area may well reflect how far we
have to go as well.

Willamette Mission State Park represents an important public hold-
ing along the river. The general area also contains a large island called
Wheatland Bar, and an adjacent large Greenway property called Grand
Island. The name of Willamette Mission State Park memorializes an early
Methodist mission, Willamette Mission Station, established by Reverend
Jason Lee in 1834. The chief goals of the mission were in line with those
of many other such settlements in North America and throughout the
world: to spread the reach of their religion, to encourage Christian settlers
in the area, and to convert Native peoples to their religion.

The goal for some, back in the 1800s, was to "Christianize" as many of
the Native peoples as possible and spread the gospel. Jason Lee and those
who traveled with him to Oregon sought to meet that goal—for indeed it
was part of their mission. I will not seek to traverse what can be difficult ter-
rain regarding the effect of such religious settlements on the first peoples
of North America; the impact is crystal clear and has been well chronicled

worldwide, whether one is looking at the history of the Amazon River Basin, the Missouri, the Willamette, or many other locations. Traders who brought disease, the military who brought force, and institutionalized racism that continued for decades are just some of the things that Native peoples have had to endure; in regard to racism and economic injustice, many still bear those burdens to the present day. The land was theirs, and it was taken from them. Further, treaties were not honored.

It is easy to understand why some Euro-American people—whether the men who completed their obligations in the Hudson's Bay Company, or the later arrivals who traveled from the eastern states by wagon train— chose to stop in the Willamette Valley. A wide-open landscape greeted them, containing favorable soils, water, and a relatively mild climate— and when they arrived the Native tribes had already been depleted by disease brought by white traders. Some of these arrivals settled near today's Champoeg state park—and the larger area known as French Prairie.

In the case of the missionaries, the physical Methodist mission is said to have been located on what is today the remnant of a long side channel called Mission Lake, which was once the mainstem Willamette. The mission, located at a high point of a vast bottomland, overlooked the river, with access for river travel and open access for those traveling by land. Most importantly for the project of the mission, they were connected to the remaining populations of Kalapuyan and other Native peoples who were left in the area.

The general area of the mission site was excavated in 1980 by OSU anthropology students, long after the original mission site had been abandoned, to determine the original location. All signs of its location at the surface of the land had disappeared in the decades after the mission moved to the Salem area to the south. In their excavation, the budding anthropologists and their professor found the site, with outlines of the original buildings; they also identified several thousand artifacts that date to the mission period of 1834–1841. Today, the side channel remnant where the mission structure was located is a shallow lake. It is easy to see that this lake was once a sizeable channel. From time to time during very high winter and spring river flows, this channel regains some of that old form and flows like a river channel.

Over time the mission ran its course, and the surrounding landscape was sculpted, cut, and pushed around to create vast agricultural lands

A view of a part of Willamette Mission State Park, looking west toward the Willamette.

around Mission Bottom—the same lands where Native peoples had once gathered food. One can view the stair-step of lands spreading from a high valley terrace in the east, then stepping down a couple of times in distinctive drops toward the river to the lowest floodplain area. Historically, as with sections of the river upstream, a tangle of side channels and backwaters spread across the bottomlands. These many decades later, the area is now characterized by thousands of acres of agricultural land that supports hops, grass seed, raspberries, and more. Whether you look from the land or by air, the view is dominated by agriculture.

On the east bank of the river, where Willamette Mission State Park is located today, the agriculture is intensive enough to leave the park itself standing, so to speak, as a relatively isolated island of green. It is also bordered to the south by a massive gravel extraction operation, with a smaller one to the north. Thankfully, across the river to the west, just downstream, additional Greenway lands exist—Wheatland Bar, Grand Island, and, just below them, Eldridge Bar Landing.

In an incomplete but perhaps meaningful comparison, the same tide that swept the Kalapuya, the Chinook, and many, many other Native peoples into great hardship is the same tide that over time degraded aspects of the Willamette River's very essence, as well as lands and waters far beyond the Willamette. While I know these are different things, they to some degree suffered from the same forces. In both cases there was a disregard for what was, and an imposition of values that have little to do with the natural world.

I cannot claim, by any stretch, a full understanding of the hardship that generations of first peoples were subject to in the Willamette Valley and beyond—the wanton racism and ill-treatment that has afflicted Native communities has been horrendous. Such racist crap is still too often seen today, in the United States, and around the world, as has been made clear yet again, in 2020. Racist treatment of Indigenous peoples has occurred for generations, in Oregon and beyond—and its elements can be seen today in the actions of both individuals and institutions. Progress has been made, but clearly there is a long way to go. Some of the books I read in my twenties—from In the Spirit of Crazy Horse and Custer Died for Your Sins, to Dee Brown's Bury My Heart at Wounded Knee, and many more fine examples in literature—all point out the obvious, which has gone on for generations.

All along, at Willamette Mission and beyond, the push of Christianity at that time was a far cry from what is truly Christian in many cases. I write as someone who does not subscribe to any organized religion, but it seems to me that ignorance, fear, and prejudice have been promoted, and have done their work over time. Thankfully they have not completed the job. People who were here generations before Euro- American people traveled to the region we now call Oregon are still here, and they persist.

So what is the Willamette mission of today? Perhaps better said, what is "our" Willamette mission today? Perhaps the mission is twofold: one of equity and inclusion for all, and one of a more robust level of ecological function for the river—and everything beyond it as well. From my riverine perspective—one that also hates injustice in all its forms—these two issues are not at odds, each having its own level of importance.

When imagining the look and feel of the historic river, I think of the ever-changing channels from season to season, a place that is frequently home to so much water that it spreads outward for miles, ushering in thousands upon thousands of spring chinook returning every spring. Myriad birds were ever-present, flying across the swirling waters, from migratory songbirds to every species of water-loving bird imaginable coming across the Mission Bottom area. Canada geese, great egrets, wood ducks, grebes, cormorants, and many more. It must have been amazing to listen to the endless calls of all these birds, spread out across the floodplain for miles at key times—channel after channel and backwater after backwater. I have described some of the key issues affecting our river system of today: lost and degraded habitat, lack of working fish passage, hundreds of square miles of agricultural fields immediately adjacent to the Willamette and its tributaries, the spraying of tens of thousands of gallons of herbicides targeted to a specific "pest" or issue that necessitates, for some, a chemical onslaught every single season, and more. Runoff from cities and the sullying of our waters by human waste is all too common. These various situations, instances, and realities sometimes leave me, a dedicated and at times very frustrated steward (among many other dedicated people), more than a bit frustrated. It seems we need to better enact a new Willamette mission.

Let's consider for a moment the definitions of the word "mission." The range of definitions for the word include some that might, frankly, seem dated and offensive. One says, "An important assignment carried out for political, religious, or commercial purposes, typically involving travel."

Coyotes old and young can flourish on some Greenway properties.

Another declares, "The vocation or calling of a religious organization, especially a Christian one, to go out into the world and spread its faith." One that resonates a bit more in relation to the need to improve habitat and be more humane might be the one from the Oxford dictionary: "Any work that someone believes it is their duty to do." This definition may be more fitting for a modern interpretation of the word mission, and for addressing the needs of the Willamette and other river systems. It can also reflect the mission to eliminate racism, prejudice, and inequality that is much-needed today. Today's Willamette mission is in need of the new definition, updated and better aligned with the definition above. It might also include the element of an assignment. Reversing harm might be at the forefront of the definition and assignment.

In the early decades of the twentieth century, pollution of the Willamette from city sewage and waste from pulp and paper mills was the central part of what harmed the river, and that reality carried forward into the 1970s, when significant improvements were made to how such waste was treated. The facilities had to make major technological improvements. Of course, at that time there were those who said such improvements would put them out of business, or would simply hurt them economically. Arguments of that type were made against the federal Clean Water Act, and other efforts as well. At the end of the day, progress kept going, and the water became much cleaner. Over time, our society has learned a lot about what healthy rivers need, and today this knowledge is being applied to the Willamette in some ways. In other ways our approach is still middling, and inadequate to the task at hand—seemingly always constrained by the pull of the dollar. In fact, some of the old arguments are heard time and again about regulation and the economic impact it is said to have on private businesses. Some things never change, it seems. At the same time, today's conversation is better informed about what is needed, and more progress is being made.

The current mission for the Willamette incorporates a number of approaches, from working to improve the condition of habitat on the main river and its many tributaries to continuing to reduce pollution from a variety of sources and reducing the impact of dams to the river system. All these efforts need to continue in earnest to enable positive change to occur for the river. A mix of advocacy, lawsuits, education, and more has allowed much of this work to increase in scale over the past twenty years.

Great blue herons flourish along the Willamette's Greenway properties.

Dealing with invasive species is another major area of action and need. In some instances, it may well be that some tough choices need to be made in terms of which species to let go and which species to address.

Today's mission is one of continued improvement and ongoing effort—though the overall success of the new mission is not entirely guaranteed. It has always been a bit of a surprise to learn how decisions are made in terms of what is prioritized for public and private funding and what is left alone. Willamette Mission State Park is an interesting piece of the Willamette River Greenway's history. As mentioned earlier, the idea of eminent domain, first put forward by workers at the Oregon Department of Transportation back in the late 1960s and early 1970s, was elevated by opponents of the Greenway proposal to a major threat, which then translated into intense political opposition. In the case of

Willamette Mission State Park, eminent domain was actually utilized: Phil Blake and his family owned property and a house on part of today's park site; his 350 acres contained a hazelnut orchard, floodplain habitat, and a beautiful setting just upstream of the Wheatland Ferry. Because it was Oregon's plan to establish five focal parks, eminent domain was used in this case. Although this practice remains an outlier, the outcome was most certainly used during that time as an example of what could happen to other properties along the river.

In the case of the Blake's, the issue went to court, and the family was paid $700,000 in 1973 for the property, which was appraised at $350,000. In a story on OPB's *Oregon Field* in February of 2013, John Blake, Phil's son, still felt bitterness and sadness about the whole episode.

In some ways the establishment of Willamette Mission State Park is a mini episode of many lands lost along the Willamette River—simply a different version of a very old story. In the case of the Blakes, they received some compensation for their loss. In the case of Native peoples in the area, and throughout Oregon, the people were not ever truly compensated in the same way, financially, emotionally, or otherwise.

Over the last decade significant work has occurred at various locations at Willamette Mission State Park to remove wide swaths of invasive species (such as Scotch broom and Himalayan blackberry) and plant native plants. As of today, hundreds of acres of habitat have been improved, and in time a greater level of connectivity of the side channel with the main river may occur as well. More active flow in the side channel in the spring is a benefit worth exploring, and worth the investment of additional restoration dollars. Such investments, both terrestrial (in terms of floodplain forest) and aquatic (with modification to the channel) can benefit a wide range of native birds, plants, fish, and more. Human diversity and ecological diversity—both are essential for a healthy world. Unfortunately, in the realms of justice and ecological health, we still have a long road ahead.

10
Assemblages

Acts of creation are ordinarily reserved for gods and poets, but humbler folk may circumvent this restriction if they know how. To plant a pine, for example, one need be neither god nor poet; one need only own a good shovel.

— Aldo Leopold, "Pines above the Snow," A *Sand County Almanac*

It took two hours to make my way across perhaps half of the big island. Equipped with a motorized trimmer with a rotating steel blade, I edged forward through the tall reed canary grass on a hot June afternoon. Boots laced tight, old work pants on, gloved hands gripping the trimmer handles — I slowly made my way through and around blackberry thickets, trees, and tall reed canary grass.

It was a weekend work effort that provided scale — and I was surrounded by nature. To the left and right the tall invasive plants towered above me across a hummocky landscape where each step had to be taken with care. Reed canary grass coated the floor of the area, interspersed with long-fallen trees and the residual rotting wood resting here and there — giant logs being slowly reclaimed into soil. Up and down, and over ridges of soil carved by the river's high flows, one had to be mindful of each step. It would not have surprised me a bit to find some deep hole that could claim an unwary person — with a poorly chosen step resulting in a fall into the depths of some long-lost floodplain trap. More likely, I'd just have to watch out a bit for the contours made by the high flows that might set a day's exploration back with a twisted ankle or similar injury.

Whirring and cutting, with my ear protection in place, the sound of the motorized rotating blade I was wielding was just a bit muted. I could only imagine that this sound was nearly as invasive to the insects, birds, and other nearby wildlife as the tall invasive weeds seemed to me. Thankfully my incursion into this landscape was temporary.

Just across from the big Willamette Mission State Park this wild island is found, part of a beautiful complex of Greenway lands: Wheatland Bar is, for the Willamette, a large island of about 170 acres. Abrasive here, beautiful there—its big tangle of willow, Oregon ash, black cottonwood, and a wide assortment of life is almost unvisited by people. High banks in many areas make easy access from the river tough, along with the layer of riparian vegetation and an abundance of large wood resting along the island's edge. The upstream end of this island has a wide-open meadow, except in this case the meadow contains what appears from the air to be two converging forces: a huge expanse of large Scotch broom on one side and, in some kind of strange ecological pose, a mass of Himalayan black-berry on the other. Both of these invasive species were large, found in hundreds of clumps, and seemed to have been well established for years.

On this late spring day, my goal had been to simply explore this inter-esting public property. Like other properties along the river, because this is an island, it is both protected to some degree and, at the same time, neglected because of the relative isolation. Tangled mixtures of plants were everywhere—and even a few wildflowers peeked out where the reed canary grass hadn't suffocated them. From years of paddling my canoe in this area, I could envision the sweet side channel on the west side of the island. Shallow and fast flowing, the side channel gives rise to another longer channel that makes its way eight miles to the west and north, creat-ing Grand Island. For the mid-Willamette River, the channel diversity in this area is unique, and something to embrace ecologically.

The Wheatland side channel is two miles long, and after the first half mile, the Grand Island side channel starts. At the opening of this channel is another public property, Grand Island Natural Area. At just shy of four hundred acres, this is a big Greenway property for the Willamette—this meshing of the large island, two side channels, and another large Gre-enway property creates an area that is ecologically diverse. Then, just upstream on the main channel's east side is Willamette Mission State Park—at just over 1,200 acres. Finally, just a half mile downstream of Wheatland Bar, another Greenway property, Eldridge Bar Landing, forms a long peninsula of green on the river's east side. All in all, this is a lot of public land for the mainstem Willamette.

Step by step, carefully avoiding yellow jackets, logs, and occasional poison oak, all the while guarding against tripping over blackberry shoots,

The upper end of Wheatland Bar in early fall. This large, fantastic Greenway property has a lot to offer the natural world.

I moved slowly upriver. I imagined that, given I was in the middle of the island, even the loudly buzzing machine would likely not be heard from the river over the sound of the birds, wind, and water. My point was to cut through a short stretch of blackberry to gain access to the interior from a Willamette Water Trail campsite. The island is owned by two state agencies: the upper end belongs to Oregon Parks, and the lower end belongs to the Department of State Lands. After about an hour I'd cleared a walkable path through the high thorny bushes. I put the trimmer down and entered the open expanse. All around was a vast array of large blackberry patches that extended hundreds of meters. Throughout, clear lines along the ground made the crisscrossing habits of various wildlife obvious. About halfway across this more open area the blackberry transitioned to a vast sea of scotch broom—clearly these two converging masses of weeds had never met a trimmer, or any other human effort to decrease their abundance.

On either side of this open area the large trees along the riverside created a border, making any view of the side channel or the mainstem river pretty tough to acquire. Overhead, two red-tailed hawks circled on the summer thermals, with an occasional call that seemed to spread through the forest. Overall the air was permeated with the sounds of bees, hoverflies, Swainson's thrushes, and the songs of other bird species—with the gentle wave of sound swirling into the whirr of the wind flowing over and through the trees. To the east, only the occasional beeping of equipment in the gravel extraction site could be heard. This was *quiet* for the mid-Willamette.

I had tied my canoe firmly to a tree, checking the knot twice. Traveling far inland away from the shoreline, only to be left wondering how well I'd tied the canoe off, was not something I wanted to experience—over the years I'd learned that lesson more than once. It is some kind of solo traveler's paranoia, to be twenty minutes away from a craft and suddenly, only then, to question whether it has been tied off properly! Uncertainty flowing in with the image of the untied craft being slowly lifted by rising water—I'd imagine making it back to shoreline just in time to see a distant image of the wayward craft far downstream. Maybe such images are relegated to those with active imaginations, but I've heard enough historical accounts of such experiences to not leave such situations to chance.

Heat settled in, as the early afternoon sun was high overhead. I'd carried some water and a couple of snack bars on this little inner island excursion. From maps I'd examined from the late 1890s, the island had not changed all that much—even in the highly manipulated mid-Willamette. In places, the steep bank on portions of the main channel side had certainly eroded away, but that is the nature of the river. I wandered to the upper end of the open area, weaving among the mature Scotch broom. It was easy to imagine work crews coming in to remove the common invasive plant, but of course, on an island, the logistics would be a little trickier—yet it was a task that was very possible to set in motion. Weed wrenches were perfect for the job: a human-powered tool, made of steel, with a grip at the base that can grab the Scotch broom just above where it emerges from the soil. A person pulls the long handle and leverages the root mass out of the ground. It is very satisfying work at times—even when a couple of tries are needed to remove the persistent plant. In this field, it would take a small crew a couple of days of hard work. Given the fact that Scotch broom seeds can remain viable for decades once they fall to the earth, ongoing vigilance must be exercised when mature plants are removed. Each spring the same area must be scoured for the many small shoots that appear. Thankfully, the small immature plants are typically easy to remove by hand, given the moisture still in the soil.

Toward the end of the open area, I spotted something strange. In between two of the cottonwood trees was some kind of structure. I made my way closer, edging along an obvious deer path that wove between the large weeds. After a few steps it was clear—a deer stand had been constructed between the trees. At times like this it is easy to get annoyed with how people take advantage of the natural world and public lands. The "hunters" had bolted this structure, constructed of stout welded steel, to the adjoining trees. Aboveground about fifteen feet, the illegal structure provided a wide view of the upper end of the island. It basically provides a vastly unfair advantage for the hunter, though such stands can be found in other areas as well. Clearly this one had had a lot of effort put into it. Although some seem to have the highest regard for what they call "private property rights," the same regard is not always earnestly applied to public lands and its rules and rights, and certainly not to the rights of the natural world.

Tree stands such as this one, which had clearly been there for some time and was likely used by a local person or group, were not permitted on Oregon Parks or Department of State Lands properties. Further, deer stands should never be permanently attached to a tree—and this one was, in multiple places, with screws driven into the tree. It was likely that these were bow hunters, given that shooting a rifle on Oregon Parks Greenway properties was illegal. It is one thing to camp, paddle, hike, and hunt along the Willamette, but another thing entirely to illegally construct a welded deer stand on public land.

A rope ladder made its way up one tree trunk, then to a permanent ladder. It was the least I could do to cut the rope ladder off. So, I did. I also notified my friends at the State of Oregon, who encouraged me to take other action. What keeps occurring to me in these situations is the general disregard some people have for basic rules. After doing a bit of dismantling, I made my way back to my canoe. Acrobatic honeybees made their way here and there across the field, and red-tailed hawks circled overhead. This place, so very close to large numbers of people, felt isolated and even wild. Back on the river, I circled the downstream end of the island and started the work of heading up the back channel. The channel is replete with vibrant riverside growth and is one of the nicest examples of habitat complexity in the mid-Willamette. In most places the water is fairly clear, and fast moving.

Canoeing against the current is a bit of an acquired art, and can be a good workout as well. The process is straightforward, really: reading the current and searching out eddy lines are the most important factors. Staying close to the shoreline—just barely out of reach of the extended tree branches, shrubs, or wood debris—usually provides a break against the main flow of the current, and even better, this positioning may even have slack water, meaning little to no current. Ultimately finding an eddy—where the water flows slightly upstream—is the ideal. Making one's way upstream is a process of stitching these features together, and looking ahead, paddle stroke after paddle stroke.

Imagine taking ten or twelve paddle strokes close to shore, then moving out into the current to avoid a log extending from the bank a few feet, then moving back into shore and finding a slight eddy created by a rock ten meters upstream. Eddies are easy to recognize after a bit of practice, and the same goes for areas where the flow is modest and a consistent paddle stroke will keep the canoe moving forward. In my case I have the advantage of a sleek, fast, solo canoe with the seat in the middle. This craft makes moving upstream in these conditions even easier. It is a repetitive process, but one that is a challenge, and actually pretty enjoyable. Once a rhythm is established, it is even possible to enjoy the sound of the birds, the beauty of the lush green of the riparian plants draped along the river's edge, and even to look to the colorful rocks on the river bottom in hopes of spotting an agate. All this effort can provide a good workout—as the sweat can start to pour after just a few minutes, depending on the conditions.

On this trip, after about twenty minutes I had made it up to a large gravel bar where the side channel calved off into another side channel that borders Grand Island Natural Area. I was now at one of the larger Greenway natural areas along the Willamette. Since on this weekend day I had no pressing time constraints, I had planned to take a bit of time to explore the property.

As I moved inland, my grandmother on my mother's side came to my mind. She loved the outside world but was not always able to experience it in the way I am able to. I think she would have loved walking along the river here, and traveling through the woods on well-trodden deer trails. It was the nature that was close to home that resonated with her, from the

Steller's jays in the spring, diving into the yard, to the raccoons who lived in a giant fir tree next to the garage. It was through her that I was first introduced to books on the natural world, from Annie Dillard's *Pilgrim at Tinker Creek* to the old *Audubon Bird Guide* I found on the bookshelf. This property had attributes she would have enjoyed.

From the Wheatland Channel, this additional channel pushed its way across a partially blocked opening and began to make its way west and then northward before rejoining the Willamette. The large island created by this additional channel is Grand Island—which gives the natural area at the channel's upper end its name. The overall island is sparsely populated and is dotted with farms, some large and some smaller. At some point, large boulders had been placed at the opening of this channel, likely in an attempt to block some of the flow from reaching the secondary channel. This channel, as well as the slightly wider and fuller side channel shaping Wheatland Bar, provided a welcome dose of diversity in this river's habitat. In this area of the mid-Willamette it seemed there was some chance to locate western pearlshell mussels, but as of yet they have not revealed themselves. A full snorkeling effort of the Wheatland side channel revealed none—only a few shells here and there. That said, more exploration is needed.

The four-hundred-acre Grand Island Natural Area is the largest wooded area on the whole of the island. Moving inward on the large morphed gravel bar, the edge of the natural area, here and there I saw pits in the gravel—some many meters in width and some a few feet deep—created by high flows and the accompanying energy of the water. Swirling and pushing and guided by the shape of the channel upstream, these flows could move even large gravel in a variety of ways. On this summer day, one of the pits contained a bit of water, and a smear of river algae at the water's surface. Another of these basins was larger but had drained and dried out long ago. It was possible that the larger gravels, with their spaces in between making it easy for water to drain, enabled this pit to easily lose volume after the high flows receded.

Soon my view encompassed one of the largest collections of wood I had ever seen. Massive cottonwood giants were turned on their sides, root wads connected to broken trunks protruding from the mix. The whole was ten feet high and eighty meters in length. Smaller branches and trees poked out of the mass, with chunks of wood, leaves, and sticks along with some more recently downed trees. The mixture, the scale, and the geometry of these big collections of trunks and root wads, along with their array of smaller pieces, is always interesting. To imagine the sheer force of the water, eroding and felling the big trees, then carrying them, often for many miles, to be deposited in particular areas where the current slows, or where eddies are formed, or where they encounter obstacles such as gravel bars and riparian forest. Then, after another high-water season, the vast artful array of wood is reshaped, sometimes carried away piece by piece or en masse. Perhaps it is not a sculpture, per se, yet these collections both large and small can have a very real natural artful beauty to them.

I climbed up on a large cottonwood trunk a couple feet off the gravel bar, enabling a good look into the interior of this mix. It is always interesting to see what else is in the mess besides wood. Sometimes the mixture of material is both fascinating and a bit sickening. At times one can find an array of trash and related debris mixed up in these large wood piles. This particular collection certainly contained the human element: in this mix of wood and human-made things, plastic was a defining human feature. Bottles of all sorts were there—most with ripped and faded labels. Some of the plastic bottles were full of yellowish liquid—they were full of urine. Anyone who has traveled on the interstate freeways in recent years knows there is a species of trucker who, instead of stopping to relieve themselves at a truck stop or rest area, decides to urinate into a bottle. Given the demands of the industry and the miles between stops, that practice can be helpful to them; the problem is some throw these bottles out of the window, onto the highway median or the roadside. As you can imagine, some must throw them off of bridges, because I've found quite a few along the river.

I recall one trip on Interstate 84 a few years ago where we saw literally dozens of pee-filled bottles lying in the median and on the roadside. Now, we all know there are well-behaved truckers out there who act like adults, but clearly there are those who simply don't care—even into 2019 and beyond. I conducted a simple internet search of the issue and was surprised. Clearly it has been happening for quite a while, with media as early as 2003 popping up on the issue. It is simply hard to understand this type of wildly absurd behavior. Where does one learn that such behavior is somehow OK?

As I walked carefully through the drift-dropped assemblage of wood on the river, you might say I was fully surrounded. It almost seemed that if

The side channel around Wheatland, to the left, calves off another channel (here seen to the right) that creates the Grand Island side channel (image looking upstream to the south).

a person fell into this kind of mix, they might never be found. But within the naturally occurring wood fortress, there was also the unnatural. Draped on one log was a diaper. Indeed, someone discarded a used diaper along the river, and later it had been swept away. I'd seen it before, but it still blows my mind a little bit. I mean, what is the point of using a diaper, for these folks? It makes me wonder about parenting—people need a license to drive a car, yet no "basics of parenting" class is required. All humor aside, it seems there are a few folks who could benefit from that. Here and there, green and blue pieces of broken plastic chairs could be seen, along with an endless array of cigarette butts, bits of old clothing, used propane fuel bottles, and a thousand fragments of plastic from unidentifiable items that had been broken down bit by bit over time. Yet always, the discarded fully smoked cigarettes. Apparently a person can have brains enough to buy cigarettes, but potentially not enough to understand that the discarded pieces are trash.

Now, I don't recount this story in the hopes of creating a sense of depression; instead, it indicates something about the job at hand. The trash and debris issue is complex, and comes from a variety of sources. A more recent issue is the large numbers of homeless folks living along the river in some cities. I've worked on this issue for years, as have many others. When homeless camps are vacated, whether in Springfield, Eugene, Salem, or Portland, often a lot of material, equipment, and waste is left behind. People are not typically in the best situation when they are living along the river, and when they leave it is often a sign of upheaval for them. Some are simply unable to deal with their belongings and discarded items. Addiction and mental health can be factors that lead to being unable to cope as well. The remedies for this source of trash and debris found in the

A mix of riverine logs and wood intermingled with human artifacts.

river are clearly complex—yet the situation on this river is a clear indication that more must be done for people in such circumstances. There are, at present (in the fall of 2020), hundreds of people camping along the river in Springfield, Eugene, Corvallis, Salem, and Portland.

If you can imagine a form of waste material, it has probably been found along the river at some point. Clearly this significant and complex societal issue occurs for a variety of reasons. At the same time, it can affect water quality, human health, and ecological health. It was ironic to be walking next to a beautiful floodplain forest in the summer sun, with the sounds of water and birds all around and yet to be exposed to such a mess.

Leaving the big woodpile behind I made my way into the forest. Weaving into the shade under the trees, the deer trail I followed sunk immediately into shade. Cottonwood giants and Oregon ash collected much of the sunlight, leaving a filtered shot of energy for the snowberry and serviceberry below. Here the floodplain forest was lush. Behind me and to my left I could still hear the flow of the side channels. Here and there birds zipped through the understory. Red-eyed, with rust and white on its front and underside and black head, back, and wings speckled with white, a spotted towhee whisked from elderberry branches low to the ground, landing on the floodplain soils. Soon I saw another nearby, with the occasional confirming chirp. Dark-hooded, saturated with deep blue, a Steller's jay passed overhead. Given the season, I could make out the quick movements of an occasional kinglet, and even a warbler or two. This forest was pretty wonderful. Though surrounded by farmland and animal-feeding operations, this island of wooded wonder gave me a sense of what the Willamette must have been like three hundred years ago.

Leaving Grand Island and its forest wonder, I headed back downstream. In ten minutes I had reached the main channel and headed downriver toward Eldridge Bar Landing. As the third part of the assemblage of properties below the mission, this long peninsula of land was similar to others on the river. At high flows it was an island, yet for the majority of the year it was a long peninsula, home to the usual arrangement of invasive weeds and native plants and trees. Like other areas, both the land and the backwater of this property abuts private agricultural land. Flowing only at high river levels, the side channel is typically full of standing water, with a bit of hyporheic flow making its way through the river rock from upstream.

Eldridge has a mixture of plants and trees that have been part of the Willamette mainstem for a very long time—the assemblage of cottonwood, Oregon ash, willow, and more. Intermixed is Scotch broom, Himalayan blackberry, and reed canary grass as well. Sometimes when I arrive at public lands like this that are coated with species of plants that make it difficult for the native ones to survive, I think about the choices people make, and the many examples of unintended consequences, such as introductions of invasive plants, that result. The individual stories of how they arrived to our shores are often both interesting and telling.

Scotch broom was introduced from Europe, where it is native, to the US East Coast, although the exact date is unknown. It was found in California by 1860 and was sold as an ornamental plant. It is said that Captain Walter Grant brought it to the Northwest—Vancouver Island, to be exact—and from there it made a rapid spread through British Columbia, Washington, and Oregon. Today, the familiar yellow flowers and dark green leaves can be seen along most every roadside in Western Washington and Western Oregon in the spring.

That long-ago desire to utilize what some thought of as an attractive plant resulted in one of the most pervasive invasive plant infestations, which now covers much of an entire region and provides a really solid example of how invasive plants have been introduced and how they can spread. It is a kind of tradition, in truth. So much of what ails the Willamette, and other rivers and lands, can be traced to poor choices regarding introducing a species to a new landscape. Here we can think of tamarisk in the US Southwest, or English ivy in the Northwest, as well as many others. Whether the introductions were purely accidental or planned, today we have a wide range of species that compete with—and often outcompete—the plants and animals that have flourished along the river for thousands of years.

Luther Burbank, a plant grower from California, is often credited with the introduction of the Himalayan blackberry. In the 1800s he marketed and sold blackberries as an easy-to-grow producer of wonderful fresh fruit. Being in this line of work, he traded seeds with people from around the world. At one point he received a packet of blackberry seeds from a grower in India; he named the plant "the Himalayan Giant" and offered it, according to historian Phillip Thurtle of the University of Washington, to the public in 1894. This was the beginning of the end!

The beautiful native wapato (*Sagittaria latifolia*) grows along many quiet spots along the river.

People in Washington and Oregon purchased the seeds, and soon enough, the Himalayan blackberry plant was showing up in yards and alleys. Soon after, it would spread well beyond the gardens of local people and expand across the temperate, coastal Northwest. This was the beginning for a plant that is now so pervasive, it is often difficult to avoid seeing it everywhere—on the borders of parking lots, roadsides, at the edge of any open field—and especially in many riverside areas. The story of Himalayan blackberry has been replicated with many other plants, both decades back and more recently, resulting in the great many species we see on the landscape and in our waters today.

Eldridge Bar has been home to both terrestrial and aquatic invasives. Along its downstream end, a long backwater can be found. If you come in the early summer, you just might see a bit of wapato growing along the edges. Visit again a few weeks later, and the wapato has been overgrown with a large expanse of ludwigia, also known as water primrose. ludwigia is a relatively new invasive to the West, and aquarium owners can be credited with its introduction to our rivers. Native to South America, ludwigia was, and still is, sold as an ornamental for use with aquariums. A quick internet search yields myriad ways to purchase this plant, from

The start of ludwigia in the Eldridge backchannel.

offerings on Amazon to local aquarium shops. Just a few years ago I'd paddle the Willamette's alcoves and side channels and see the parrot's feather aquatic plant, also invasive, but subsurface and typically not filling a whole channel. Today, the reality for these backwater areas is much different. Now, a July paddle into these areas can be very tough, as many are completely choked with ludwigia. Bright yellow flowers on vibrant green shoots can be seen everywhere, in dense assemblages. Often you can't see open water because of the plant, let alone the native wapato, which may have been visible a month earlier but by July has been overtaken by the invasive. In some instances, you might see the triangular leaves of wapato poking just above the ludwigia. In the span of just a few years, this fast-spreading aquatic weed has covered more than a hundred miles of the Willamette River.

Ironically, side channels and backwaters are important components of river health—often providing habitat that can be a refuge for a range of species, from western pond turtle to cutthroat trout. At times these areas are infused with cool groundwater that can provide essential habitat in the hot weather months when the mainstem Willamette is elevated in temperature. Now, with the arrival of ludwigia, the very water chemistry can be changed, and temperatures may even increase. Dissolved oxygen can be lowered, and formerly ideal conditions in such areas can become something much different for native fish.

Like many invasive plants and animals, the solutions for removing or dealing with ludwigia are far from perfect. Herbicide applications must be made—in water—or mechanical removal is possible in a small percentage of sites. Unfortunately, mechanical removal is not always possible because of permissions needed from local landowners and the sheer logistics of getting vehicles into some sites. Additionally, if just a sprig of this material makes its way downriver, it can recolonize new areas quickly.

In the summer months, Eldridge's back channel plays host to ludwigia, ever pervasive along the slow-moving backwaters below Junction City. Over the years this seventy-acre property has received little attention, and it shows. Much of the upland portion of the property contains a tangled mess of both native and invasive plants. One of the adjacent farmers does nice work and has an environmental bent. Camping there can be very enjoyable, with a beautiful site on the lower end—necessitating paddling up the backwater during summer flows, with the effort rewarded with a short few steps up the steep bank to a large campsite replete with the sound of wind and water.

This being said, in time, the owner of Eldridge—the Oregon Parks and Recreation Department and partners—will hopefully be able to gain

A vast expanse of the invasive ludwigia clogging a backwater area.

the resources to conduct some level of habitat restoration work. This property is nice, yet it is perhaps the least of the assemblage within a couple of miles of Wheatland Bar and Grand Island. Even so, if you take some time here on a spring day, you may be deeply rewarded by an array of migratory songbirds, from the common yellowthroat and Townsend's warbler to numerous woodpeckers making their way among the trees. If you hit it just right, you will hear the moving water and rippling leaves on a mid-spring day, and the sound of bird life all around. Such days and moments provide one of the truest expressions of why riverside natural lands are essential.

11
Challenging Traditions

> The prospect of a general and permanent lowering of environmental
> resistance becomes grimly and increasingly real with each passing year
> as the number, variety, and destructiveness of insecticides grows.
> — Rachel Carson, *Silent Spring*

Only a few miles down from Wheatland Bar, the river is noticeably different from what is found upstream. Quick currents that are a hallmark of the upper Willamette are nearly gone, appearing only around a few gravel bar islands. The same can be said for the miles of river below Albany. Most discernible is the increased turbidity of the water. All the particulates from thousands of square miles of farmland and urban runoff add up. Add to that the influx of treated wastewater from municipal treatment plants and the picture is clear—the water is carrying a heavier load.

I've traveled this stretch of river many, many times. Like other riverside areas, many of these miles are characterized by gravel extraction in places where the hum and rumble of machinery can be heard (along with the ever-present beeping of vehicles backing up) for much of the day. In some ways these uses are not in keeping with the idea of natural areas set aside for public enjoyment—but clearly that has seldom figured into decisions regarding permitting for gravel extraction, or anything else, for that matter.

Farmland of various sorts is also present on this stretch, as the river winds at the edge of one of the premier grape-growing and wine-producing regions in Oregon. It also has a few remaining Greenway sites. Yamhill County is on the west side of the river and Marion on the east, with Clackamas County farther north on the east side. Around the backroads on the east side of the river, hops are a prominent agricultural crop. They are easily distinguished from other crops by the thousands of poles and lines erected to enable these viny flavor agents for ales and lagers to climb skyward. To the west, hops and vegetables of assorted varieties are also grown, as well as an influx of hazelnuts, which are being established seemingly by a hundred acres a week. All of these intermix with the vast amount of property supporting vineyards as one reaches the nearby hillsides.

As in other areas, manure can be smelled from time to time — part of the land application from combined animal feeding operations (CAFO). Imagine a dairy, with little land for the animals to actually roam freely on. There they are fed and milked — often many hundreds of them, relegated to one site. Endless gallons of manure are generated from the cows, and that manure is typically placed into a large lagoon. From there the manure is loaded into tanks and sprayed onto adjoining fields. In other cases it is trucked away to be sprayed elsewhere. I understand that the generation of most any food can produce waste, but at times there are real problems with our current prevailing methodology for producing dairy and other products.

For one, when the waste is applied in large quantities its stinks — often profusely, and can affect large areas around where the application of manure is occurring. In Oregon, the US EPA has delegated authority to administer the federal Clean Water Act to the Oregon DEQ, which is a common occurrence nationwide. Then, the DEQ transferred authority to the Department of Agriculture in Oregon, to administer the program for agricultural permits. Such permits set a range of guidelines for how CAFOs operate, including the level of manure application to the land. Typically such permits require that the application of liquid material occur when the air is most calm — seeking to restrict the travel of the smell of manure — and set specific conditions for the ability of the soil to assimilate the waste.

These practices, which have been growing in the last twenty years, are refined a bit from time to time. They are tweaked, or made slightly more palatable to the general public and the environment, but generally large amounts of liquid manure are applied to the land regularly. There is a need to get back to some of the past traditions that saw a greater balance in agriculture, with smaller scales of operation making more sense for the land and water. Instead, today we often have many animals in small areas generating a massive amount of poop, which is often then applied to the land — and often close to waterways. One can hope for the best set of conditions possible to break it all down in a way that provides nutrients to crops and creates healthy soils, all without polluting conveyances for water or forcing neighbors to live in constant stink.

At times I've witnessed the yellowish, foamy streaks traveling down-river in some areas, while during the same instances the smell of cow manure pervades a multi-mile stretch of river. Yes, this is a problem—and one tracked to more recent traditions. I know some good agricultural producers in the Willamette Valley, people who care about clean water and about the intersection of agriculture with a healthy river system. I also know well that there are those who work at an industrial scale in how they approach the land—with some seemingly disregarding rules and updated practices and making the sheer volume of waste hard to manage.

At times there is little that is green in how Oregon implements the Clean Water Act. It is not a natural situation to have the Oregon Depart-ment of Agriculture (ODA) both promoting "agriculture" across the board yet also being the agency responsible for enforcing the rules to protect the water, land, and air. The whole situation doesn't pass the sniff test, so to speak. Yet, as we've seen in other areas, agricultural companies and their associations control a lot of money and, as a result, command a significant amount of influence over regulation and enforcement. In this area, the situation is very clear historically—although some agricultural operations are doing great work, we can often do better in protecting clean water and healthy habitat.

I recall a time a few years back when a local landowner called the ODA to lodge a complaint related to water quality and a local fish kill. A "fish kill" is when multiple dead fish appear, typically floating at the surface of a water body, which is not usually a natural occurrence. In this particular instance, he noticed dozens of fish dead in a small pond adjacent to the Willamette, which received runoff via a local ditch. He called the agency, identified the adjacent landowner, and asked that ODA come out to investigate the site and the overall issue with water quality related to the application of manure on the neighboring property. In this case ODA responded, but gave the landowner three days' notice before they would show up to conduct a site investigation. The conversa-tion went something like this: "Yep, that is a valid concern, sir. Well, we contacted the landowner, and today is Monday, so we plan a visit to his property on Thursday." To say the least, the person lodging the complaint was flabbergasted.

In the same vein, because of the fish kill witnessed on the water by the neighbor, the Oregon Department of Fish and Wildlife was contacted as well. ODFW went out to the site, saw the dead fish (which consisted of a few trout, smallmouth bass, and crappie), and indicated they would contact ODA to determine a course of action. In this case, both of the agencies failed to take action. When ODA visited days later, the landowner in question had adjusted the scene enough to warrant only some recommended actions from the agricultural agency. Indeed, this has been a fairly routine state of affairs in the history of enforcement in the greenways of Oregon. Even with the best of practices, at times the will to implement the remedies for waste and for the protection of our land and water seems to pale against tradition. The tradition here is that, over time, agricultural interests have exercised a lot of control over what occurs—from decisions regarding simple ways to document the application of herbicides to tens of thousands of acres of land annually to the ability to establish more meaningful riparian habitat "buffers" along streams and larger waterways.

Claims that agricultural interests are the true "stewards of the land" are too often a far cry from reality. Although there are some outstanding people and agricultural producers of a variety of crops in Oregon, there are enough strange actors and historical actors to pollute that particular narrative in robust terms. Existing regulations are also questionable and are far too lenient toward those who are conducting business as usual.

Traditions come in a variety of forms. In the past few years I've encountered individuals who seem to hold to some interesting ideas about tradition. To generalize, for sure, in some areas along the river private property rights are spoken of with great reverence by some landowners—as they should be. At the same time, in other areas of the river, such notions are disregarded as long as an individual gets what they want. River access is one such issue. I've encountered a property that recently changed ownership when a nonprofit received the property from a private landowner. What was clear from the get-go was that adjacent landowners were at times using the property to gain access to the river—all the while without the permission of the owner, or the previous owner. Access from land was prohibited at this property—the nonprofit owners preferring to have the area in a natural state, with access only by boat—but some of the adjacent folks who lived nearby continued to enter the property by land, trespassing all the way. This reality was pointed out to them numerous times, but while they spoke of "the importance of private property rights," that notion didn't prevail when they wanted to continue their traditional, unlawful practices. You see, it seems that for some it is human nature that dictates their actions and stated positions—if they have been trespassing on someone's land for years, it is hard for them to stop. Unfortunately, this kind of thinking occurs regularly in a small fraction of people.

Two years in a row, one person who had become accustomed to trespassing actually entered the property with a tractor and cut a combination of native and invasive plants down, all in an effort to make it easier to hunt for ducks on the property later in the year. The last time this occurred, the county sheriff was called by the land manager and the person 'fessed up, saying they would not do it again. Interestingly, this is a person who would publicly extol the vast rights of private property owners, and how defying the rights of private property owners was against the foundation of the nation—and other such related pronouncements. Those who speak of paddlers and river users trespassing seem at times to be seeking to cover up their own misdeeds. The same holds true for some people who cut down trees on Oregon Parks lands, or let their farm animals graze in Greenway properties along the river. I hate to say it, but we've seen this a few other times along the Willamette and far beyond. It is an interesting trend, though thankfully, most people do not behave that way.

Downstream, a few miles above Newberg Pool, is a beautiful property known as the Sanctuary; a Department of State Lands island, nice in its own right, is just upstream of the Sanctuary. The Sanctuary property is a big inside bend, at about river mile 63–65. Once an agricultural property, and adjacent to two others that were agricultural until the late 1990s, most of it is now under a federal watershed easement—an earlier version of the conservation easements provided by the federal government.

Today the Sanctuary property is held by Willamette Riverkeeper and is managed for conservation and low-impact recreation. The main work at the property is centered on efforts to control invasive weeds, as well as efforts to establish native plants. It also happens to have a Water Trail campsite and a long circular path on the interior. With access open to low-impact use—typically canoes, kayaks, and drift boats, it makes a nice addition to the Greenway. Properties like this—held by nonprofits, open to the public, from the water in this case, yet conserved for natural habitat—are a great addition to state-owned Greenway properties. Over the span of a couple of years I've spent quite a few nights at the Sanctuary. From rain-drenched weekends in December and January and icy-cold blue sky winter days to star-filled spring and summer nights, the property always engages the visitor in nature. It might be viewed as a key component of the final assemblage of undeveloped, publicly accessible areas for camping on the lower sixty miles of river.

I recall multiple nights, listening great horned owls hoot and call to each other from upriver to down. At times one of these owls would land so close to the tent that it may as well have been perched in the tent vestibule. In the spring, juvenile great horned owls can be heard. A kind of persistent shrieking is evident, followed closely by the *hoo, hoo, ho hoooh* call of the adults. It may be the same young one moving about the floodplain, up and down the river, with an adult close behind. In this way the juveniles seem to be led out into the world, chaperoned by the adults.

Another of the many species found in the Greenways.

Making their way through the night, the juvenile learns how to detect their prey and successfully feed in the bright moon and in the shadows of cottonwoods.

Bald eagle, osprey, and red-tailed hawk fill the sky at times there—as do scrub jay, Steller's jay, varied thrush in the winter, and an assemblage of migratory songbirds in the spring. The forest understory is replete with Swainson's thrush in the late spring and summer, where they have found the low floodplain forest with its relative warmth a refuge against the colder temperatures of the mountains. Experiencing the sound of the flowing river, the whirr of wind through the trees, and the long mornings replete with birdsong of every type is immersion in the essence of this riverside land's long history.

A couple of years back, I discovered a large, old empty hundred-gallon barrel of an herbicide called Dinoseb on the property, in a low point in the property that fills with groundwater when the river is high. This discovery reinforced the reality that this floodplain peninsula was once a major agricultural site where chemicals were commonly used. At that point I'd never heard of Dinoseb, but a quick bit of research revealed that that particular product was a chemical compound that was found to be quite toxic. In particular, it was highly toxic to fish if it entered the water. Like other pesticides, Dinoseb was once used widely to kill unwanted plants of all kinds. Fortunately, in 1986 some level of collective wisdom came forth, and this product was banned in the United States. Even so, somehow it is said this substance is still likely used in China, based on tests of rain and drinking water. Hopefully common sense will prevail there as well.

This discovery really hit home for me. It is easy to imagine barrel after barrel of this substance being mixed with water and applied to the landscape with little thought—all to kill unwanted plants that might compete with the vegetables grown on the same ground, at the same time. Such an approach to agriculture had likely gone on at this property for decades and reflected tradition.

Some of these substances—whether for urban home use, suburban landscape use, or agricultural widespread use—have negative impacts on a range of species, both plant and animal. What I mean by this is that chemical substances utilized to conveniently eliminate one form of life may well have impacts on other forms of life. Instances of the unforeseen

An aerial view of the big inside bend Greenway property owned by Willamette Riverkeeper known as the Sanctuary.

consequences of our thoughtless chemical manufacture and use are wide-spread in the world, and certainly apply to the health of water, air, and land. Yet it seems a bit absurd to use the word unforeseen, when in many cases, the effort to take the time for even a minimal evaluation of potential consequences has historically been tepid at best. The effort to actually see, and learn from what we see, can be quite constrained.

Tradition seemed a strong theme in the general area of this Greenway property. It was a small outpost amid what looks to be a sea of agricultural land in Yamhill County. To the west a massive assemblage of cows at a concentrated facility are producing milk—evidenced by the strong smell of manure at times in the early mornings. The brownish-yellow mix is commonly spread onto nearby farm fields, with giant sprinklers jetting the liquid refuse onto the soils.

To the north is an assemblage of gravel pits, some long unused and others still being excavated. To the east, at the height of the steep rise, more grass seed farms can be found, yet many of these fields have been recently transformed into hazelnut orchards—all dictated by the world market for these nuts. Hazelnuts, or "filberts," are known well to those of us who grew up in Oregon and nearby. Most people likely know one of the global uses of this nut in the sweet, chocolatey spread called Nutella. With a recent blight in Turkey, the world's largest hazelnut producer, many landowners have eagerly transformed their former cropland to hazelnuts. Seemingly everywhere one looks in the Willamette Valley, the recent installation of tiny hazelnut trees can be seen on former grass seed and other fields. Soon these diminutive starts of only a little over a foot in height rise to several feet within a few years.

Perhaps most present for the river traveler is the nearby highway, which comes close to the river's edge at this site, pretty close to the top of the cliff face to the east. About half the time the prevailing westward movement of air helps buffer the incessant sound of cars and trucks moving north and south along this highway, while other times the noise has no restriction and wafts outward and across the property. Perhaps in time the open field at the top of the rise will be planted with hazelnut trees, creating a bit of a noise barrier. This may be one lesser-known benefit of the rapid transition of fields to orchards in the Willamette Valley—the slight buffering of noise from vehicles and more. Sure, complaining about the sound of traffic in the Willamette Valley may seem foolhardy to some, yet what one experiences along the river says a lot about who we are, and what we *all do* in this world. It also speaks to what we've become used to in everyday life, sensical or not.

On a bright note, not long ago I was just downstream of the Sanctuary, traveling the side channel around Candiani Bar, which is a large island owned by the Department of State Lands a few miles above Newberg. Rich with native trees and shrubs, Candiani is an outlier in the Willamette River portfolio of properties owned by the DSL. Over the years I'd trekked here and there on this long curve of island. It is definitely a unique property, especially along that relatively low stretch of river just above the Newberg Pool. With a farm to the east, and no other large Greenway properties downstream for several miles, the forest of this island is a small stronghold. Willow, Oregon ash, massive old black cottonwoods, and a host of native plants make up Candiani's forest. Bald eagles fly over regularly, and red-tailed hawks nest in more than one location high in the cottonwoods. The whiff of nearby traffic in Newberg can at times be heard if the wind is right, and small planes sometimes practice landings and takeoffs on the island's large gravel bar on the mainstem side of the property, but in general the place feels peaceful and wild.

On the upper end of the mainstem, just across from Candiani, is another DSL island—smaller and lower, but cradling another sweet side

Long and varied, Candiani Bar—owned by the Oregon Department of State Lands—is a large island with a sweet back channel that hosts myriad wildlife, including a few western pearlshell mussels.

channel with some very nice habitat. The shallow side channel of the summer months is replete with the sounds of birds and insects—all woven together with the swirl of the gently flowing channel. In August I took the Candiani channel to head back to San Salvador Park by canoe. After a few minutes I stopped at a small eddy, after one of the few areas with quick current, to take a moment to listen to the birds, the wind pushing through the shimmer of green leaves in the trees all around, and to have a bit of my water. After examining the verdant forest for a minute, hoping to get a closer view of the raven that had just flashed overhead, I looked down into the shallow water. I immediately did a double-take: there on the border between the fast-flowing current and the eddy was the blurry but unmistakable image of a freshwater mussel! I got out of the canoe and walked carefully into the water, scanning the river bottom. With a hit of joy and surprise, I found several more in the same area, perfectly snugged into the substrate. I carefully lifted one up out to the water to assess the general size. It was at least five inches in length—an adult indeed. I placed it back in the substrate, just as it was.

Over previous months of snorkeling for mussels over a wide area, I had frankly written off this stretch of the river for this species. It just seemed to be too burdened by multiple issues to support western pearlshells or floaters. Also, I had examined the stretch between Salem and Wheatland and the long channel behind Wheatland Bar, which seemed ideal for mussels, and had found nothing. Assuming that mussels downriver would be unlikely, looking farther the previous year had not been a priority.

Seeing these creatures so far downriver in the system provided a sense of hope—and a desire to continue to look in areas that seemed less likely to have mussels. Not long after, my friend Eric and his daughter traveled down the side channel behind Five Island, a couple miles upstream of Candiani. He found several large adults on that side channel as well. Soon after, I paddled my canoe upstream to that island from San Salvador Park and counted a nice group—not a very large or dense group, but definitely present. It was a meaningful reminder on mussel biology and distribution, and a welcome sign of the surprising persistence of western pearlshells. Although the State of Oregon may not do enough to prevent pollution from coming into the system, and habitat had been degraded, seeing these mussels in the Willamette provided a sense of hope: resilience and persistence were factors to consider in looking at the ecological health of the river. Piece by piece the losses to the river's ecological fabric might be reassembled with grit, hard work, intelligence, and passion for what might be possible again.

12
Fairfields

> We paddled into this place not knowing what to expect. We spent two
> nights here and it was simply amazing. The peace of the river, the
> sound of the birds, and the beautiful trees and blue sky—this greenway
> is such an amazing gift.
>
> —Mary, logbook at Eldridge Bar campsite, 2019

I paddled in my canoe, north of Salem, a few miles downstream of Willamette Mission State Park. Somewhere up off to my right, to the east, a two-lane highway was facilitating traffic between Salem and Newberg. Like other two-lane highways east of the Willamette, this one is not all that far from the river, or that far from Interstate 5. With increased population and the development of travel apps, this highway now plays a central role for a lot of people in their daily travels. It always has, but now there are just simply many more people using it. Thankfully, only occasionally could I hear a vehicle off in the distance.

The morning was overcast, but the warm day would come after a morning of cool clouds—typical of many Willamette Valley spring and summer days. Early summer had the birds whisking about in the riparian fringe and larger floodplain forest parcels. I was the only river traveler in view, and at that hour, I had not seen anyone else on the river. It was simply gorgeous. The dip of my canoe paddle in and out of the water and the chatter of migratory songbirds were the sounds surrounding my passage along the river. On this morning the occasional great blue heron and ever-present osprey could be heard as well. It felt as if every creature living in that space and in that moment had some elemental understanding of the beauty of that place, and the beauty of the morning. Sure, anthropomorphizing other living things can be a slippery slope, but all the same, that is how it felt.

On this stretch of river, I had already passed by the verdant Wheatland Bar, and every time I do I decide to make a mental note to get back there soon, just as I do with other Greenway properties I haven't walked around on in a while. It was the Willamette—big, complicated, and beautiful. There the full array of resident and migratory birds could be found, and the property was large enough for all manner of river valley wildlife, from bobcat and coyote to deer and beaver.

Along this stretch were other properties as well, even some with a couple of forested areas that are private. I was aiming for a private parcel I had permission to travel on and visit that had grown on me of late, and likely always should have been pretty interesting to me. In prior weeks I had explored it quite a bit, given permission by the landowner to look things over. It has all of the constraints, contradictions, and complexities of many Willamette floodplain lands. It also had an abundance of ecological strengths that could provide a solid base for the river's future—yet only if more such properties were added to the mix from south of Eugene to Portland. Along those lines, the efforts to purchase, preserve, and restore habitat on the Willamette need to be augmented. Islands of green against the sea of urban nodes and the agricultural expanse need to increase—for the many reasons already discussed. The state and nonprofit groups need to up the game; hopefully we are on the cusp of the next fruitful chapter for the Greenway program.

Here along the river, a stretch sometimes forgotten, gorgeous combinations of native floodplain life are found. From giant black cottonwoods that almost seem to strain against their natural lifespan, holding fast to gray rounds of river bottom and sediment, to verdant rushes of snowberry with their tiny white bead-like fruit and myriad serviceberry and Nootka rose, all visible depending on the season. All of these can be found along the Greenway. Sometimes an island, and other times a long peninsula, this property looks much the same as it is depicted on maps more than one hundred years old. Even affected by the surrounding world, this little property was a wonder.

In addition to the natural beauty and elements of natural habitat, one can find aquatic weeds in the dead-end back channel (alcove) and many other invasive weeds—the vast majority with seeds arriving on high river flows, across a good portion of the property annually. In essence, this property is Willamette River cup-half-full, with all the usual challenges included. Notions of possibility and potential are interwoven in this one place, all of it steeped in the reality of the ecological fabric along the

river that is so very manipulated from decades of human impact. Here
the words intervention, influence, and activity might be substituted, yet
"impact" seems the most appropriate in regard to the human effect on the
landscape. Historically, the adjoining area, called Fairfield, was a small
community started in the 1850s that was blessed with a ferry landing that
provided passage for agricultural goods and people up- and downriver. The
small town was at the top of the bluff, which protected it from flooding.
Fairfield was small, but obviously significant for the surrounding agricultural area, according to historical accounts.

After about forty-five minutes of paddling, I neared the long peninsula
and backwater. Only occasionally could the distant whirr of a motor vehicle zipping along the highway be deciphered. Overhead the birds continued their pursuit of insects amid the humid, windless morning. Rustling
to my left, a small creature caught my eye, a silhouette of riverside avian
watchfulness. Dark, then slightly green, a small heron whisked upward
from the river's edge. Green heron to the core, the creature gave nothing
to chance, having likely seen me a good hundred meters or more upriver,
but biding its time until I was still multiple canoe lengths upstream. It
gave a short alarm call, but flew only another five meters, landing on an
easy foothold at the edge of the silty left bank. Cautious and not always
seen, unlike its larger cousin along the Willamette, the green heron has a
more distant sensibility, and its population is less concentrated along the
river than the great blue heron.

It flew up, and soon landed again just ahead on a riverside log, a few
meters from the shoreline. From time to time, like this one, green herons
will wait and allow you to pass by in close range, which can afford a sweet
view of this interesting bird. Dark crested at the top, with the feathers on
its head seemingly spiked upward and penetrating yellow eyes, this one
decided to wait, and simply watched me pass by. Perhaps the quiet cues
of my canoe paddle gave it a bit of pause instead of triggering its defensive
mode.

In this moment I was appreciative of the nearby riparian fringe, a bit
wider than the norm found along much of the riverbank, and certainly
glad that there was a larger floodplain forest habitat here that covered dozens of acres. Green islands, verdant islands, essential islands—all these
nodes of habitat constituted a small line against the surrounding land
use that extends for miles. For birds, fish, amphibians, and mammals,

these irregular borders of green are critical. For people as well, such space affords a view, little human noise, and an opportunity to mesh with the natural world. This is what has been lost along most of the river, and every effort to gain some back is critical.

I pulled the canoe against the mixture of sand and rock that formed the gentle beach on the downward tip of the island. Securing the rope against a nearby ash tree, I walked along the shoreline. Typical of the Willamette in early summer these days, already a bit of algal growth could be seen along the water's edge. A small opening between the tip of the peninsula was the exit point for a long backwater. This narrow bit of water separated the end of the long peninsula from vehicle access from the adjoining property.

After a few minutes of walking the shoreline, it seemed to me this place had not been visited for some while. A year before, a person had been living on this property, cutting down trees, lighting large fires, and basically making a mess. Although the property is a private one, as in other instances, some people don't always heed "no trespassing" signs, or the fact that some areas are intended to be for wildlife and quiet

Three deer walk in the floodplain forest.

contemplation. This property had suffered the same fate as others, historically, with people trespassing, cutting down trees, hunting, driving vehicles into sensitive habitat, and more.

Back at my canoe, I pointed it up the backwater. It took only a couple of minutes of paddling to reveal the heron rookery. Composed of nearly sixty nests high in the cottonwoods, this home to herons was active with adult birds feeding the young herons that had hatched only a month and a half before. The atmosphere was squawking and loud, the whole area full of adult and juvenile birds moving about. All told, the rookery was spread across several large cottonwood trees, vibrant and very well established. At times rookeries diminish because of birds of prey feasting on the young birds or human factors making an area less attractive to the large birds. This one was very big.

Watching the activity at this rookery, it was not hard to see the connection these large birds had to their distant ancestors. From their movements to their loud calls and various forms of guttural chatter, I could almost imagine them as pterodactyls tending their young. Given the proximity of the nearby highway, which they could likely see from their perch, it was good to know that this rookery seemed to be thriving.

A cedar waxwing, a migratory songbird, perches among the riverside ash trees.

With a few more minutes of paddling, it was evident that bird life on this property was in full swing, with a mix of beautiful neotropical migratory birds zipping around in the lush green mix of native plants and trees. Away from the cackling of the heron rookery, the full mix of birds could be seen and heard on this property. I made my way to a small opening in the forest canopy and got out of my canoe. Soon I was on the small one-lane service road that circled the property. All around the sounds of warblers, kinglets, and bushtits could be heard. I could hardly keep up with my binoculars as the small forms—gray, black, and yellow—could be seen.

As I walking along the lane that wove its way among the green of the cottonwood, Oregon ash, snowberry, ninebark, Nootka rose, and other native plants, this private Greenway property gave testament to the necessity of such areas. At about ninety acres, the floodplain expanse gave me a sense of hope for wild things, and for he wildness of the river.

Surrounding this property, the push of mechanized agriculture was all around. Of course these operations produce needed goods, yet at times, unfortunately, the intended and unintended consequences of how things have been done in recent decades tells the tale: chemical inputs, manipulation of the soil, and workers who generate so much of the yield often exposed to inputs that have questionable outcomes for human health. It would seem that some degree of anger should be directed at the very systems of watershed manipulation that have wrought a landscape replete with toxic chemicals, rivers that no longer flow in a natural way, forests reduced to a mere patchwork of trees, and the resulting impacts of those changes on creatures that have called this landscape home for thousands of years. That is the real problem.

The name "Fairfield" exemplifies some notion of hope, goodness, and richness. Many good people out in the world are demonstrating how to farm in a fashion that is more natural. Whether one subscribes to Wendell Berry's approach to agriculture, or the myriad variations that can be seen today, *there are options*. Approaches that do not rely on chemicals can be better for the soil, as can changes in approaches on tilling, or considering whether to till at all. I've looked back to Rachel Carson quite a bit in the last decade, and her acumen and warnings about the chemical onslaught were amazing. It would seem that there are enough red flags to spur greater change, and greater action—yet even so, change is very slow.

Over the past couple of decades, I've met the mavericks of agriculture in Oregon, and they are good people. I've also met the apologists who would have us believe that anyone wearing jeans, boots, a button-up shirt, and the right hat is somehow deemed sacred by the powers that be—all with an aim to just "get along." Lacking a backbone has never prevented some people from being promoted to decision-making authority over the years.

I write this as someone who grew up in Oregon, yet I've traveled and lived in other states and have had the luxury to travel to multiple countries. I also write this as a person who has had the very unique opportunity to learn about, travel, and experience the Willamette River on an ongoing basis for more than twenty years. We as a society seem to be trending in a direction that places less value on experience, and perhaps more value on youthfulness, specific demographics, and sound bites. But I also believe that there are many people in the world—of every age, ethnicity, and background—who understand my frustration with the status quo. We must improve, for the long-term health of the river and, frankly, for the planet. The notion may seem dramatic, but at present we seem to be the very scourge that may well end us.

13
The Craft

> There is one thing I should warn you about before you decide to get
> serious about canoeing. You must consider the possibility of becoming
> totally and incurably hooked on it.
> — Bill Mason, *Path of the Paddler*

In tune with the sounds of rippling water, with the wind breathing through
the riverside forest—a canoe paddle enters the water in a quick, quiet
slice. Sleek and long, the canoe hull moves quickly through the gentle
current of the river. Ancient, effective, and peaceful, this mode of travel
has been proven for millennia.

Over and over, the paddle is melted quickly into the water, pulled
backward, and sliced back up from the water, to race again forward and
repeat its entry into the aqueous realm. Over and over, and the craft is
pulled forward. The approach is ancient. It is one that also has many
benefits. In this way people propelled themselves across the water for
thousands of years. Down massive rivers for hundreds of miles. Across vast
lakes, and along oceans for days on end.

Moving a paddle craft across the water all depends on a rather simple
implement in your hands, one that simultaneously brings the essence of
freedom to the forefront. What is striking, though, is that this way moving
across the water is little-known to a great many people. That reality may
be shifting a bit. It seems today that a slow but growing wave of people
are bending toward such craft. It might be curiosity generated from a
photograph, a book, or video. Perhaps a friend relayed their experience
canoeing for a day. It may be instinctual for some when they get on the
water, and feel the movement of the hull across the surface, borne only
of your own power and that of the moving current. Traveling in this way
is real, effective, healthy, and of course it can often be very fun. In all,
the outcome described in the Bill Mason quote that opens this chapter

is a very real possibility! The legendary Canadian conservationist, artist, filmmaker, and canoeist was certainly afflicted by the canoe compulsion.

Luck has played a part in my experience over the last twenty-five years in regard to paddling canoes and other craft. Decades back, I made a few good connections with some folks who were fully immersed in canoeing and kayaking, and that connection made the difference. I sought out some knowledge and got lucky enough to have some folks help me out pretty quickly. Of course, people of the "paddle clan" are typically eager to get other people involved. I'm sure the same can be said of those immersed in model trains, mountain climbing, painting, and more. If you put yourself out there, opportunities may present themselves. The point is, if you want to learn something, frequently routes to make that happen will present them-selves that are pretty obvious. In my case it was about taking the time to explore, and being willing to endure some level of risk on a variety of rivers.

The opportunity of being able to figure out the benefits of canoeing and related forms of paddling has been great. Whether researching the how, the what, the when, or the why of the paddling pursuit, I was able to jump into it on a personal and a professional level. I recognize that not everyone has such an opportunity, where personal and professional lives mesh to some degree. I've always found it interesting that people seldom attribute some level of their good fortune to sheer luck. I certainly think luck plays a part in many things, and one has to recognize that.

Since canoeing gripped me years ago, in the professional world I and others have sought to bring the barriers to engaging human-powered river travel down to the lowest possible level. The goal is to enable anyone who wants to take part in experiencing the river in a human-powered craft to have an opportunity. It seems to me that getting people on the water—whether standing on a stand-up paddleboard, sitting in a kayak, or paddling a canoe—is essential to connecting with something different from everyday life and with the natural world. Over time, such adherents can become more attuned to the needs of clean water and healthy habi-tat. Frankly, when you are a paddler, it is easy to be an advocate for the wild, for clean water, and for the health of the natural world.

I cannot recall how many times someone has said to me, "Wow, I had no idea. This is totally cool, and my perspective of the river and nature is totally different." Yep, that is a common statement heard all over after a first paddle trip. Utilizing human-powered craft creates a different

Two canoes glide across the river's surface.

atmosphere and seems to help the individuals taking part gain a different sense of their presence, along with their vulnerability. Such experience also speaks to the ability of a wide array of people, with different capacities, to take part. A reverence for the power of water and the power of nature is also a pretty common feeling for many people traveling rivers and other water bodies in such craft.

In supporting human-powered travel, I am not opposing motorized river travel. A power boat can be a very useful tool, at times, and can be used safely and appropriately in many areas. At the same time, our reliance on motorized "everything" seems to have gone to a very strange place. Seemingly every day one can view an outsized pickup truck that requires a small ladder to get into. What is the point of that? You seldom see such trucks hauling anything of substance. Likewise the range of motorized watercraft, which seem to speak to some primitive part of the human brain in their never-ending whirr or slow, gas-guzzling plow to create artificial surfing waves. Some machines just don't make much sense in some places in the modern era. From noise and pollution to their impacts on habitat to the sheer use of natural resources to fabricate them and make them run, such machines are out of step with modern times on a number of fronts. If one wants to surf a four-foot wave, then go to ocean beaches for goodness sake! Get some exercise! Enjoy the natural world! Artificial waves are not fit for inland waterways unless they are created on very large water bodies that generate wind-driven waves naturally, and on a regular basis.

Thankfully, there are very real, time-tested alternatives for river travel that are much better for human health. Some forms of travel may be viewed as antiquated, tiring, hard, difficult, or time-consuming, and generally challenging as well. The canoe may well fit into that mold for many people focused on their little electronic screens these days—young and old alike. At the same time, the rewards of moving a canoe through the water, many miles down a river, across a lake or other waterway, are many. It is a practice, an art, a sport, and a discipline with many benefits. This description fits other kinds of paddle craft as well.

So, what is a canoe, you ask? A canoe is an ancient form of paddle craft, and very well represented in North America. Perhaps best first represented in the Northeast United States (with more modern recreational forms appearing similar to the original craft of the Algonquin people and other Indigenous peoples of the Northeast, present-day United States and Canada), the birchbark canoe is beautiful, refined, and emblematic of centuries of river and lake travel. The bark of birch trees was the skin of the craft, and it was fitted with ribs that helped to sustain the shape. The birchbark canoe was created with great expertise, using the natural materials available many hundreds of years back. Other similar forms could be found historically across North America, from the Midwest to the West, as well as in other parts of the world, though the way such craft were created differed from place to place.

Northwest Native peoples utilized canoes widely, primarily dugout canoes made from whole logs. Such dugout canoes were used, and are used, from the coast of Oregon far up the coast of British Columbia. Both large and smaller versions of these canoes could be found on inland waters as well. Some canoes were crafted for large groups, others suited for just a couple of people. In most every instance these vehicles were crafted to meet the needs of the users in a particular place. Use of canoes in the Willamette River system is pretty well documented. One account in 1836 by botanist David Douglas tells of a village on the Santiam River a short distance from its confluence with the Willamette River, with, "plenty of canoes." Other historical evidence points to canoes being used throughout the Willamette River, and especially on the lower reaches of the river.

With dugout canoes, a whole log is utilized for one canoe. Over time the interior wood is carved out to reveal the basic shape of the hull, while at the same time wood is scraped from the outside of the log to further delineate the elongated shape of the canoe and to create the overall shape. Hot rocks were used to create hot water and steam inside the log to patiently stretch the fibers outward, thus widening the interior space. Variations on this type of approach were used for the large canoes used on the Columbia River and other coastal bays and estuaries for hundreds of miles.

A style known on the upper Willamette and in other places in the Northwest is the shovelnose canoe. These smaller craft, for one to three people, were used to travel, hunt, fish, and gather from. They were dugout canoes, but low to the water, and with a bow area that was wide and open, with a gently sloping platform look. An excellent example of this style of canoe is found at the Confederated Tribes of Grand Ronde's Chachalu Museum and Cultural Center. That particular craft was discovered in 1980 after a flood on the North Santiam River, which eroded away enough riverside soil to uncover this wonderful craft. The Grand Ronde have put significant effort into their Canoe Family, building new dugout canoes over the past decades, and getting their youth into the craft and into learning how to paddle and travel. Further, they and other Northwest tribes regularly get together and take a canoe journey of varying lengths in the summer, continuing their expertise and tradition and passing this on to the next generation. Such experience will only help to continue the building and use of traditional canoes well into the future.

The journals of Lewis and Clark also describe the canoes of the people at the mouth of the Columbia River. While the accounts certainly testify to the craftmanship of the canoe, even more was their focus on the proficiency and expertise of the paddlers. The Chinook people could move these large and elegant dugouts through big water, dealing with wind and waves in a very dynamic physical environment. Members of the Northwest tribes were, and are, experts with these craft. After watching a group of Chinook in a canoe paddle through some very tough conditions, William Clark remarked in his journal that they were "Certainly the best Canoe navigaters I ever Saw."

Given the history of these craft, it is quickly apparent that they are perfect for traveling rivers, lakes, and bays, far and wide: from the nearly two hundred miles of the Willamette River to small rivers and creeks to large

Fully loaded for a long trip, this canoe can travel hundreds of miles if needed.

estuaries and bays to lakes found anywhere in the world. In canoes of the
past few decades, there is typically room for one, two, or three people—
depending on the configuration—in each craft. There is also ample room
for gear, and space to stretch out your legs as well. Most importantly, there
is the opportunity and the ability to move quickly through the water with
the current, using one's muscles.

Over the past couple of decades, literature about canoes in North
America has been on the rise, and at present is varied and rich. A trip back
to the Canadian Canoe Museum in Peterborough, Ontario, in the early
2000s was eye-opening for me. Crisp, clear, and with myriad examples of
these craft, the museum brought a sweet light to the history of the canoe
and kayak, from their use by the first peoples of North America to all those
who embraced the craft after. Certainly the use of the canoe by European
settlers and those who came after to exploit vast tracts of land owned by
Native peoples is problematic and complicated. That is a fact. Yet, the
story of the ingenuity and expertise displayed by first peoples in develop-
ing, building, and utilizing these craft is pretty amazing, a story now richly
described in books and video. These craft were tools indeed—very critical

tools for survival. They often also evoke high levels of craftmanship and wonderous artistic achievement.

Today on the Willamette, the options for paddling these craft are many, and the public lands along the river speak to a sense of openness and freedom for those who choose to try. The Greenway properties are essential to this experience.

When I first paddled a canoe as a kid, I was not completely convinced of the majesty of these small boats. At the same time, it was not something I was able to do all that much. Later, in my twenties on the Willamette, I was able to borrow a canoe, a PFD, and a couple of paddles, and I was immediately hooked. It was primal, but also understandable; paddling a canoe for a couple of hours on my own, I was captured by a sense of freedom and a feeling of possibility as I made my way down a stretch of the lower Willamette River. Freedom is the principal notion that arises—to glide along the water and see the world around you and experience the nature of a river or lake. Paddling to the left for a few strokes, then to the right, then back to the other side. In a few minutes you see the place where you started your journey fall quickly behind you, as the winding river unfolds ahead of you. At one point I recall feeling an odd sense of regret at the years behind me that I'd never prioritized getting out on the water, whether the Willamette, the John Day, Columbia, Clackamas, Waldo Lake, Netarts Bay, or many other water bodies in Oregon and beyond. It seems to me that when you feel that sense of unused time in your personal history related to a new activity, you must truly love it.

From a physical standpoint, a wide range of people can paddle a canoe (or kayak or standup paddleboard). After the sometimes cumbersome job of getting the canoe to the riverside or lakeside and back if it is an older, heavier craft, once it is in the water it moves rather easily. Today, with the advent of much lighter materials for construction of canoe hulls, many weigh forty-five pounds or less. The average person or couple can easily lift such a craft to walk it to the riverside, tow it with a bike trailer, or load it onto a vehicle.

Given the big river's moving water, and lack of rapids, the Willamette is a perfect river for those new to paddle craft and river travel, as well as for seasoned people who just want a bit of tranquility. Some of the Greenway properties along the Willamette are great entry points to the river, and these properties can also make fantastic rustic campsites.

Although this book has been critical of some of the State of Oregon's green ways in relation to official Willamette Greenway properties, many areas lend themselves to healthy habitat, a bit of peace, and low-impact river travel; multiple small natural areas along the river can be peaceful and full of wildlife, and visiting them is a great way to get away from the normal pattern of everyday life.

Spending a few days on the Willamette and other rivers is also a pretty healthy way to exist, and for most people, the act of paddling a craft along a river for a few to many miles, setting up camp, and conducting the basic camp chores that make a trip work are simply good for the human body. While some people do have movement limitations that may reduce their ability to paddle a canoe or kayak, for those who can work their way into such recreation, the benefits are many.

As a type 1 diabetic myself, exercise is pretty important to me. I've had this chronic chore of a disease since I was six, so finding ways to maintain my health has been key. While regular exercise such as running, weight-lifting, biking, hiking, swimming, and more are great options for anyone with this condition, it didn't take me long to figure out that traveling along the Willamette in a canoe, camping, and doing some physical riverside work was simply *great* for managing the disease as well. That such activity would be helpful is intuitive, to some degree, yet at the same time I was surprised these activities could be that helpful, given their lack of intense cardio. It is more about the frequent movement when outside, on or along the river, that makes the difference.

Moving from the canoe to the shore, carrying camp gear, setting up a tent, setting up the camp table, sunshade, and other camp materials means that a lot of physical movement occurs. Simple, direct, and frequent, the movement around camp and along the river burns energy, which is essential to keeping blood sugar in the appropriate range. Adding up the many tasks over a day makes the benefit pretty clear. Although there is certainly some down time while camping—relaxing in a camp chair or hammock, enjoying the sights and sounds of the river—it is the relatively frequent movement that makes the difference.

Whether gathering firewood, setting up camp, breaking down the camp in the morning, repacking the canoe, or the act of paddling itself, all the energy burned during these moments does the trick. Then, when I add on walking a trail on some Greenway property, doing a bit of work to

Perfect craft for the perfect campsite.

remove invasive weeds with a metal-bladed weed whacker, or doing trail maintenance with the same machine, those additional physical activities go even further for my health. This is true for anyone, whether a type 1 diabetic or the more prevalent type 2.

The link between outdoor activities and the overall health of people is not a new notion at all, but the connection has gained credence in recent years, especially with the advent of the ever present "screens" in our lives. Over the past several years the concept of getting people outside more often, especially kids, has been written about a lot. Programs have existed for decades to get people outside, from kids to adults. The newer emphasis has led to additional programs and organizations being started to further engage all people in nature, and projects have been implemented to better enable access to nature, and the outdoors. Whether a terrestrial trail or river access points, these simple amenities enable people to engage in the natural world with greater ease. In fact, providing these amenities in areas that are close to where people live has been a focal point for governments and organizations—a very obvious concept that provides multiple benefits. Enabling greater access to the natural world is a growing trend, closely linked to health and longevity. This is one of the main benefits of the Willamette River Water Trail, a series of access points, natural areas, and camp sites that facilitate river travel and are well explained on the related

All along the river, the beauty
just jumps to the fore.

website and maps (www.willamettewatertrail.org). It is all about getting to
the river and going somewhere—whether for a short hour-long trip or a
multiday expedition.

An additional benefit of low-impact, human-powered travel is that,
once people get out there and explore nature, most gain an affinity for
creating and protecting such places. This is true of small city natural areas
as well as large tracts of national forest, and most certainly applies to the
Willamette's natural areas. Once they get out in a paddle craft and see
what the river offers, whether for only a couple of hours or over a couple
of days, people gain a connection to the river's offerings.

If you have never taken the time or found a good opportunity to get out
there, I encourage you to do it. Many online resources can help facilitate
your journey, whether you want to gain instruction, find equipment, or
join a club that takes regular outings. Take a few minutes to search out
paddling and instruction options or go to www.willamettewatertrail.org
and the links on that page, and as always, leave no trace. See you out there!

14
Looking Ahead

Belief is the wound that knowledge heals.

—Ursula K. Le Guin, *The Telling*

In more than twenty years of work on the Willamette, it has become clear to me that Oregon's sense of "greenness" far outpaces the reality in daily experience. A clear proving ground for this statement is the Willamette River. From pollution of different types to the abundance of habitat that has been destroyed or modified over the decades, the river has some significant ailments that affect the health of river species. If Oregon wants to begin a broader chapter of establishing greener ways of being, then the Willamette Greenway program provides a key opportunity and proving ground for how to move forward into the next few decades. There are also opportunities for all of the natural resource agencies to reduce pollution and improve habitat.

One of the most glaring needs for the Willamette is to invigorate the effort to purchase land from willing sellers along its floodplain and that of its key tributaries. This is an opportunity for the State of Oregon to raise the bar. Instead of more people living along its shoreline, the river needs to regain more floodplain habitat, and the same can be said for most of its tributaries.

As a reminder, if we think in terms of a circulatory system, with the myriad channels representing freshwater arteries, too many of them have been blocked, over and over. Not surprisingly, the result of the myriad blockages has been a more fragile, less robust river system in comparison to what existed in decades past. As a result, the most glaring need for the river—in addition to curbing toxic pollutants generally in our water, air, and land and improving fish passage at the US Army Corps dams—is to gain back some of those floodplain lands, to be owned by the public, conservation organizations, and land trusts.

What I mean by this is that we should buy up some percentage of agricultural land along the Willamette and return most of those acres to natural habitat. Given the tens of thousands of acres of agricultural land in the Willamette Valley, there should be ample opportunity to purchase a hundred acres here, fifty there, and 1,200 over there from those seeking to sell their lands. Given the mass of agriculture in the valley at present, we are talking about only a small percentage of that overall acreage.

In this vein, the State of Oregon can take a leadership role in providing funding and helping to leverage funding from other sources. Over the past fifteen years this has been done in regard to funding for habitat restoration in the river basin, yet the focus on acquisition has been too limited. Instead, other priorities brought in by outside forces have diluted some of the effort to gain back tangible pieces of property. All the same, the opportunity still exists, as generational change in land ownership continues along the river. For Oregon's leadership, here again is another chance to at least make a lasting commitment to a kind of activity that can provide long-term ecological benefits, as well as recreational benefits. This is a very direct approach to help the state regain its green ways along the Willamette, and its overall green approach.

If you examine any aerial photograph taken in the last fifty years, you will notice there is no shortage of land being used for agriculture, along the Willamette and far beyond—no shortage whatsoever. In many cases such lands occupy what was once productive habitat for a range of fish, birds, amphibians, mammals, and more. If you were to rise up a couple hundred feet into the air in most places along the Willamette River, you would see miles and miles of agricultural land all around, and only the thinnest line of riverside forest here and there. That is the reality, and it is something that is easy to see.

Statements about keeping land "in production" are simply contrived to help some interests keep power; they provide nothing back to the health of the river or to water quality or to the myriad species that make their home in riverlands. Natural production is just as important in many areas— meaning the ability of natural, ecologically healthy, floodplain habitat to sustain the natural world, with its myriad invertebrates, birds, amphibians, mammals, and fish. All of those depend on healthy habitat, free of pesticides and herbicides. It seems that so many of our current issues related to environmental health, and human health, center around similar concepts.

Adding Greenway properties and floodplain lands over the next fifty years is essential for the long-term health of the river and its communities.

Realistically, we have lost the simplicity of the natural order. Although some insects or diseases can be damaging to some crops, it would seem the pendulum has swung too far in one direction—to say the least—in terms of chemical use. In the face of fungi, unwanted insects, and other potential ailments to crops, we have created a massive industry of chemical manufacturers with the sole purpose of killing things.

Here again, Oregon can take a more robust role in creating better regulatory programs to protect the health of wildlife and people. The use of chemicals in Oregon, presently injected from seemingly every angle, can be decreased with thoughtfulness, solid alternatives, and clear intent. What seems very clear is that over time, private business interests have won out against the true needs of the natural world—look at climate change, endangered species, human health, and more. Today, along the Willamette River and so many other rivers, we find very vivid examples of this reality. Along most every river in Oregon, we need more healthy riverside vegetation and floodplain habitat, habitat that will only help our river systems, and the communities that surround them, be more resilient in the face of climate change.

It can be argued that, over the next fifty years, the emphasis should be on continued acquisition of riverside lands along the Willamette, and along many of the Willamette's tributaries—in tandem with a vastly decreased use of chemicals of many types. Given the projected rise in population in the Willamette Valley, coupled with new variability created by global climate change, establishing more natural floodplain land along our rivers is essential to the long-term survival of the rivers and the communities that surround them. As we add these lands for the health of habitat, a parallel opportunity is provided for people to engage with the natural world via canoe, kayak, raft, drift boat, rowing shell, standup paddleboard, bike, wheelchair, and, of course, book and shoe. Engagement and experience are key, and it seems that this engagement is essential to long-term human and ecological health.

So, what is the land acquisition goal for the floodplain lands along the Willamette in the next twenty years? Perhaps we can shoot for a thousand acres a year as a conservative investment on the mainstem river and its tributaries? This can be taken on by nonprofits, and by state and federal natural resource agencies. Keep in mind, all the property owned by Oregon

Floodplain forests are essential for long-term river health, and human health.

Parks in the Willamette Basin totals just over 13,000 acres—along a two-hundred-mile stretch of the river. If we used $7,500 per acre as an average, that would mean we'd need a $7.5 million dollars investment annually. In the grand scheme, this is a modest goal (of course, depending on what kinds of land a river is passing through, the estimate per acre can be more or less). Perhaps three thousand acres a year is possible, or even more.

What I am proposing here is to gradually acquire active farmland and convert it back to varying forms of natural habitat that existed centuries prior. Over the past fifteen years we've been generally spending about $4 million per year for easements and acquisitions along the Willamette and its tributaries. Easements will continue to be an important component of improving the river's health, but to get serious about having the Willamette regain its ecological health, and to gain resilience in the face of climate change, we need more land to be purchased for conservation. Such lands can also be a critical buffer against the rise of more frequent floods in the basin, slowing the rise of floods and absorbing more of the floodwater.

The opportunities are real. One can find agricultural listings on a regular basis, with properties large and small being offered for sale. In some cases, a portion of such properties could be sold, and turned to conservation—the point is, there are multiple ways this change can occur. If these investments are not made, what is the ecological and societal cost for the long term? This includes the ecological cost to many species of wildlife. This includes clean water, and cool water. This includes the ability to better recreate along the river, which in turn can help sustain healthy populations of people. To date, even the most "robust" efforts have clearly invested too little, and have had too little imagination. This needs to change.

When I am in my seventies, if I'm lucky enough to get there, I'd like to be able to take a twenty-mile hike along the Willamette River, through natural areas in the heart of the valley, varying not more than a half mile from the river at all times. At present, this simply is not possible. I may be able to get nearby the river at times, but a contiguous trail does not exist. In most cases a person seeking to take such a hike would be walking along a two-lane road or highway.

Imagine that original Greenway goal, of a linear assemblage of publicly accessible lands along the river stretching for many miles from north to south. This should once again be the goal. This notion is not so grand—it

A large swath, by Willamette standards, of Greenway—more is needed!

is something that is necessary, and tangible. Recalling the bold historic accomplishments related to the environment in Oregon, and nationwide, places formulating a plan to make such a linear assemblage of lands along the Willamette River within the realm of possibility. Frankly, we should see such expanded assemblages and connections along a great many rivers, resulting in increased river health, increased health of wildlife, and certainly increased health of people.

Take this as a reconditioning and reapplication of an idea that has been around for a good while. In my view, the time for another bold proposal, and related plan, is *now*.

Imagine the ability to travel to the Willamette River, pack your paddle craft of choice, or your hiking boots or shoes, and to get away for a few days. You could paddle from Eugene to Albany, or perhaps hike from Champoeg state park and, crossing occasional roads, hike south to Corvallis or beyond. Sure, not an easy lift, but one that could benefit the river for the long term, and benefit a great many people.

We also need to do more about decreasing pollution—from enforcement to policy and more related to cleaning up already polluted sites, such effort must improve and expand. At the Corps dams and other dams that plug much of the Willamette River's tributaries, we must improve fish passage and, in some cases, consider major rebuilds. Over time, especially as these old projects get even older, we should consider opportunities for removal, given that most of these dams have exceeded their design lifetimes. Increasing and improving habitat, reducing the pollution that still plagues the Willamette, and reducing the impact of dams—these are the continued needs over the next few decades.

It is time to make additional change occur, and to make a push for continued improvement, embracing a renewed and expanded effort for our greenways. While my effort, and that of others who have been doing this work, is certainly not over, it is heartening to see younger folks jumping into the fray—and many of these people seem to have a similar passion for the natural world.

It is my hope that new generations of people will gain and maintain that green root in their being and help to continue to make progress on many fronts. Hopefully we will see that root grow, to support a vast tree that embodies a new era of green ways.

Selected Bibliography

Bauer, Webb Sterling. 1980. "A Case Analysis of Oregon's Willamette River Greenway Program." PhD diss., geography, Oregon State University.

Boyd, Robert, Kenneth Ames, and Tony Johnson, eds. 2013. *Chinookan Peoples of the Lower Columbia*. Seattle: University of Washington Press.

Dow Beckham, Stephen. 2018. *The Willamette Falls Fishery: Tribal Use and Occupancy, Treaties, Reserved Rights, Adjudicated Claims, and Tribal Fishing in the Modern Era*. The Confederated Tribes of Grand Ronde Community.

Gascho Landis, Abbie. 2017. *Immersion: The Science and Mystery of Freshwater Mussels*. Washington, DC: Island Press.

Grossman, Elizabeth. 2009. *Chasing Molecules: Poisonous Products, Human Health, and the Promise of Green Chemistry*. Washington, DC: Island Press.

Haag, Wendell R. 2012. *North American Freshwater Mussels*. Cambridge, UK: Cambridge University Press.

Heinselman, Miron. 1996. *The Boundary Waters Wilderness Ecosystem*. Minneapolis: University of Minnesota Press.

Jennings, John. 2002. *The Canoe: A Living Tradition*. Richmond Hill, ON: Firefly Books.

Jennings, John, Bruce Hodgins, and Doreen Small. 1999. *The Canoe in Canadian Culture*. Toronto: Natural Heritage/Natural History Inc.

Johnson, Charles. 2012. *Standing at the Water's Edge: Bob Straub's Battle for the Soul of Oregon*. Corvallis: Oregon State University Press.

Kesselheim, Alan S. 2012. *Let Them Paddle: Coming of Age on the Water*. Ann Arbor, MI: Fulcrum Publishing.

Liguori, Jerry. 2005. *Hawks from Every Angle: How to Identify Raptors in Flight*. Princeton, NJ: Princeton University Press.

Maser, Chris. 1989. *Forest Primeval: The Natural History of an Ancient Forest*. San Francisco: Sierra Club Books.

Mason, Bill. 1988. *Song of the Paddle: An Illustrated Guide to Wilderness Camping*. Richmond Hill, ON: Firefly Books.

McPhee, John. 1975. *The Survival of the Bark Canoe*. New York: Farrar, Straus, Giroux.

Meyer, Kathleen. 1989. *How to Shit in the Woods*. Berkeley: Ten Speed Press.

Nealy, William. 2000. *The Nealy Way of Knowledge: Twenty Years of Extreme Cartoons*. Birmingham, AL: Menasha Ridge Press.

O'Brien, Michael, Richard Crossley, and Kevin Karlson. 2006. *The Shorebird Guide*. New York: Houghton Mifflin.

Olson, Sigurd. 1956. *The Singing Wilderness*. New York: Alfred A. Knopf.

Rubin, Rick. 1999. *Naked Against the Rain*. Edgmont, UK: Far Shore Press.

Strayer, David L. 2008. *Freshwater Mussel Ecology: A Multifactor Approach to Distribution and Abundance*. Berkeley: University of California Press.

Williams, Travis. 2009. *The Willamette River Field Guide*. Portland, OR: Timber Press.